Victorian Nonconformity

Angel Street Congregational Chapel, Worcester
(from *The Congregational Year Book, 1860*)

Victorian Nonconformity

David W. Bebbington

CASCADE *Books* • Eugene, Oregon

VICTORIAN NONCONFORMITY

Cascade Books
A Division of Wipf and Stock Publishers
199 W. 8th Ave., Suite 3
Eugene, OR 97401

www.wipfandstock.com

Typeset by Anthony R. Cross

ISBN 13: 978-1-61097-305-2

Cataloging-in-Publication data:

Bebbington, D. W. (David William), 1949–.

Victorian nonconformity / David W. Bebbington.

xiii + 70 p. ; 23 cm. Includes bibliographical references and index.

ISBN 13: 978-1-61097-305-2

1. Dissenters, Religious—England. 2. Great Britain—Religion—19th century. 3.
England—Church history—19th century. 4. Dissenters, Religious—Great
Britain—History—19th century. I. Title.

BR759 B39 2011

Contents

Preface

This brief account of Victorian Nonconformity was originally published in 1992 as an introduction for students of history. Although not venturing far into doctrinal issues, it also turned out to be useful to those pursuing theology and religious studies. It is now reissued with updated bibliographical references and a small number of minor revisions. I am grateful to Cascade Books for being willing to republish the book under its imprint and to Anthony R. Cross for preparing the index.

David Bebbington
Stirling

CHAPTER 1

Identity and Division

Victorian Nonconformity has commonly received a bad press. Chapel-goers have been seen as narrow and censorious, contemptuous of what makes life worth living and critical of those who want to live life to the full. In *Culture and Anarchy* (1869) Matthew Arnold depicted Nonconformists as addicted to a mixture of 'disputes, tea-meetings, openings of chapels, sermons'.[1] They knew nothing, he claimed, of the 'sweetness and light' of true culture. Likewise Charles Dickens poked fun at the vulgarity of the ministers who shaped their way of thinking. Stiggins in *Pickwick Papers* (1836–37) and Chadband in *Bleak House* (1852–53) are ignorant, pretentious and utterly hypocritical. The mainstream literary tradition treated Nonconformity with a remarkable lack of sympathy. Subsequent generations have been too much swayed by stereotypes created during Victoria's reign. Wondering what once went on within the walls of a chapel now turned into a furniture store, they have too readily believed what litterateurs of the age chose to describe without pausing to question their stance. Powerful religious convictions were distasteful to Arnold; Dickens was drawing on a long-established literary tradition that held up Dissenters to abuse. Both men were expressing disdain for those they regarded as social inferiors. Like many other Victorian writers, they betray a certain instinctive aversion to a community that was often suspicious of fiction.[2] Consequently our image of Nonconformity has been distorted. The chapels, it is true, generated a way of life that was distinctive, but not one that was necessarily obscurantist or self-righteous. A delight in sermons may not be universal, yet neither is it a symptom of tastelessness or humbug. Chapel values were designed to differ from those of the public house or high

---

[1] Matthew Arnold, *Culture and Anarchy*, ed. J. Dover Wilson (Cambridge, 1932), p. 58.

[2] Valentine Cunningham, *Everywhere spoken against: Dissent in the Victorian novel* (Oxford, 1975).

society or even the Church of England. Victorian Nonconformity was an attempt to create a Christian counter-culture.

Who were the Nonconformists? They were those Protestants who dissociated themselves from the church recognised by the state. They did not conform but dissented—and so at the beginning of Victoria's reign were normally called 'Dissenters'. By its end they were beginning to prefer the term 'Free Churches', a phrase that suggested positive principles rather than negative protest against the Church of England. During much of the Victorian period, however, the description most favoured by Congregationalists and Baptists was 'Nonconformists', and Methodists, Unitarians and the various other Protestant groups would often acquiesce in the term. Technically Roman Catholics were also Nonconformists from the established church, but the faithful owing obedience to the see of Rome could not endure so parochial a label. In Scotland the word 'Dissent' was often similarly used in the early nineteenth century to describe Protestants—largely Presbyterians—outside the Church of Scotland, but the term 'Nonconformity' never entered common parlance north of the border. So Nonconformity consisted of the chapel-goers of England and Wales, with outposts in the Isle of Man and the Channel Isles. In 1901 they formed something like 15% of the population.[3] That proportion, however, comprised both members and adherents, a crucial distinction. Only members took on rights and responsibilities in their congregations; adherents, often more numerous than members, simply attended services and activities. The hard core of a chapel was much smaller than its congregation. In principle and often in reality, membership implied a high level of commitment: an MP would hurry back from Westminster each weekend to teach in his provincial Sunday school. Nonconformist church members were commonly people of deep conviction.

Their principles, in most cases, derived from an Evangelical worldview. The Evangelical Revival of the eighteenth century had fanned the embers of English-speaking Protestantism into a blazing fire. Preachers had carried the gospel up and down the land, planting Evangelical religion in parish churches as well as in the chapels. Evangelicalism had permeated society by the opening of Victoria's reign, reshaping attitudes to piety and philanthropy,

---

[3] James Munson, *The Nonconformists: in search of a lost culture* (London, 1991), p. 11.

science and business.[4] There were four main features of
Evangelical religion. First there was conversion, the crisis
associated with turning from sin to personal faith. Although not
all Evangelicals could identify the time of their conversions,
many went through acute psychological troubles before the
moment of release. 'Conviction, contrition, wrestling in prayer,
and mighty struggling', it was said of a Bible Christian from
Devon converted in 1859, ' — these were the prelude to the happy
day when the peace of God first became his blest possession'.[5]
Secondly there was activism, a commitment to spreading the
experience of conversion to others. In 1848, a typical year, a
Primitive Methodist preacher travelled 3,484 miles, chiefly on
foot, paid 1,790 family visits and preached about 400 times.[6]
Although evangelism was the priority, activism readily spilt over
into care for the sick and the deprived. The two — gospel work and
social concern — were rarely divorced in the Victorian era. There
was, thirdly, a love for the Bible. The family Bible would be
given the place of honour in the parlour, working men would save
up to buy scriptural commentaries and pins might be stuck in the
pages of a Bible to mark divine promises. 'I likes the New
Testament', declared a female agricultural worker in Oxfordshire:
'you see it is so plain. I can understand what Paul, and Peter, and
John says.'[7] And, fourthly, there was a concentration in doctrine
on the atoning death of Christ on the cross. In 1837 the Baptist
Union urged its churches to 'keep the cross of Christ ever in
view'.[8] By his sacrificial death, Evangelicals believed, Christ had
saved them from sin and, ultimately, from hell. The cross was
therefore the fulcrum of their theological system. Conversion,
activism, Bible and cross — these were the leading components of
Evangelical religion.

---

[4] Boyd Hilton, *The Age of Atonement: the influence of
Evangelicalism on social and economic thought, 1795–1865* (Oxford,
1988).

[5] W. J. Mitchell, *Brief Biographical Sketches of Bible Christian
Ministers and Laymen*, 1 (Jersey, 1906), p. 79.

[6] *Primitive Methodist Magazine*, February 1850, p. 66 (James
Garner).

[7] J. Stephenson, *The Man of Faith and Fire, or, the life and work of
the Rev. G. Warner* (London, 1902), p. 183.

[8] *Account of the Proceedings of the Twenty-Fifth Annual Session of
the Baptist Union, held in London, May 1, 2, 3 & 4, 1837* (London,
[1837]), p. 30.

Not all Nonconformists, however, were Evangelical. Chief among the exceptions were the Unitarians, the elite of Nonconformity. Unitarians had parted with orthodox Christian teaching about the Trinity in order to insist that God was one and only one. Jesus was not God and his atonement was not the kernel of their theology. William Gaskell, a leading Unitarian minister in Manchester and husband of the novelist Elizabeth Gaskell, preached a sermon in 1847 against 'Some evil tendencies of the popular theology'. Evangelicals, he contended, 'want a Redeemer who will set them free from the power of guilt, while they look on without effort'.[9] True religion, he held, called for persevering moral exertion in response to the Fatherhood of God. While appealing to the Bible, he criticised the notion of conversion. Gaskell and his denomination were far from the Evangelical position. So were some smaller groups. The New Church, or Swedenborgians, were followers of the eighteenth-century Swedish philosopher Emanuel Swedenborg, whose speculative interpretation of the Bible included the belief that Jesus was to be identified with God the Father. In 1851 there were fifty Swedenborgian chapels, many of them in Lancashire.[10] In the same year there were as many as 222 meeting places of the Latter-Day Saints or Mormons, but most of this body soon emigrated to the United States to build up the kingdom of God in the deserts of Utah.[11] Later in the century there were Theosophists,[12] Christadelphians[13] and Labour Churches[14] (led mainly by Unitarians) who also formed part of the unorthodox sectarian fringe of Nonconformity. Most would not have

---

[9] William Gaskell, *Some Evil Tendencies of the Popular Theology: a sermon* (Wakefield, 1847), p. 11.

[10] Robert Hindmarsh, *Rise and Progress of the New Jerusalem Church in England, America and Other Parts*, ed. Edward Madeley (London, 1861); D. M. Thompson, *Nonconformity in the Nineteenth Century* (London, 1972), p. 150. Other figures from the 1851 census are taken from this source.

[11] P. A. M. Taylor, *Expectations Westward: the Mormons and the emigration of their British converts in the nineteenth century* (Edinburgh, 1965).

[12] W. S. Smith, *The London Heretics, 1870–1914* (London, 1967), pp. 145-64.

[13] B. R. Wilson, *Sects and Society* (London, 1961), ch. 12.

[14] K. S. Inglis, *Churches and the Working Classes in Victorian England* (London, 1963), ch. 6.

classified them as Nonconformists at all. The Unitarians, however, were remarkable in being anti-Evangelical and yet at the heart of historic Dissent. It is with the Unitarians that a survey of the diverse landscape of Nonconformity may begin.

CHAPTER 2

Diversity and Co-operation

Dissent traced its origins back to the seventeenth century. During the Commonwealth Presbyterianism had triumphed. The Church of England had been re-organised on Presbyterian lines: bishops had been abolished; all ministers were treated as equal. In 1662, following the restoration of Charles II to the throne and bishops to the church, those ministers who could not accept the new dispensation were ejected from their posts. Many gathered congregations outside the Church of England; and most were Presbyterians. During the eighteenth century their successors, swayed by the influences of the Age of Reason, gradually abandoned Trinitarian orthodoxy. By the early nineteenth century many of these 'rational Dissenters' were prepared to call themselves Unitarians.[1] Although their origins were mainly Presbyterian, they differed totally from the Presbyterians of the nineteenth century—essentially Scottish immigrants who brought their orthodox religion to the major cities, together with Northumberland, and who in 1851 possessed 160 places of worship and 0.2% of the population.[2] The Unitarians were of comparable strength, with 229 chapels and 0.2%, but were spread rather more evenly over the country. Their city centre causes, such as High Pavement in Nottingham or Mill Hill in Leeds, were dominated by prosperous business and professional families with a powerful civic spirit whose Dissent was usually hereditary. Yet a wide social range was to be found amongst them. In Lancashire a rationalist schism from Methodism had brought over a substantial working-class membership.[3] There was a steady

---

[1] R. K. Webb, 'The Unitarian Background', in Barbara Smith, ed., *Truth, Liberty, Religion: essays celebrating two hundred years of Manchester College* (Oxford, 1986).

[2] A. M. Drysdale, *History of the Presbyterians in England* (London, 1889), part 3; S. W. Carruthers, *Fifty Years, 1876–1926* (London, 1926).

[3] H[erbert] McLachlan, *The Methodist Unitarian Movement* (Manchester, 1919).

inflow of recruits dissatisfied with the dogmatism of their former denominations. In one Manchester suburban congregation at the end of the period, about 60% of the worshippers were drawn from non-Unitarian backgrounds.[4] One great attraction was the teaching of James Martineau, professor and then principal of the denomination's Manchester New College, a message at once deeply intellectual and inspiringly spiritual.[5] Doctrine, however, was too vaguely formulated to operate as a firm ideological anchor, and many Unitarians drifted away either into free thought or into Broad Church Anglicanism.[6] There was no disguising the decline of the denomination by the opening of the twentieth century.

The Independents were equally part of the Old Dissent. Oliver Cromwell, as many Victorian members of the denomination loved to recall, had been one of their body. Unlike the Unitarians, the Independents had retained their grasp of Calvinist theology during the eighteenth century, though modifying it as the century wore on. Christ, they believed, had died only for an elect group, but, since preachers did not know which of their hearers were predestined for salvation, the gospel must be proclaimed to as many as possible. Fired by the expectation of far more conversions than previous Calvinists had thought possible, the Independents of the early nineteenth century fanned out over the country in vigorous evangelism.[7] The denomination was transformed from a string of introverted meeting houses huddled away in obscure corners like Lantern Yard in George Eliot's *Silas Marner* into a thriving network of chapels placed prominently on main streets. East Anglia, Wales and parts of the South and Midlands became strongholds. By 1851 there were 3,244 places of worship drawing 4.4% of the population—a body more than twenty times the size of the Unitarians. A new name was coming

---

[4] Ian Sellers, 'Spanning Victoria and Edward: two urban ministries around 1900', *Transactions of the Unitarian Historical Society* 20 (1991), p. 51.

[5] Ralph Waller, 'James Martineau: the development of his thought', in Smith, ed., *Truth, Liberty, Religion*.

[6] E.g., Owen Stinchcombe, 'Elizabeth Malleson (1828–1916) and Unitarianism', *Transactions of the Unitarian Historical Society* 20 (1991), pp. 59-60.

[7] D. W. Lovegrove, *Established Church, Sectarian People: itinerancy and the transformation of English Dissent, 1780–1830* (Cambridge, 1988).

into use. The title 'Independents' had drawn attention to their distinguishing belief that each fellowship of believers should be independent of all external control, whether by bishops or presbyteries. Increasingly, as they co-operated in area associations for the spread of the gospel, they began to prefer the word 'Congregationalists'. There was no change of principle, but the emphasis was now on the responsibility of the members of the congregation, gathered in Church Meeting, to govern themselves. A Congregational Union to which churches throughout England and Wales could affiliate was established in 1831.[8] Manufacturers and shopkeepers dominated most Congregational chapels, often being elected to positions of lay leadership as deacons, but skilled working men and their families were also well represented. Congregationalism, declared Robert Vaughan, chairman of the Union in 1846, 'aims to form intellectual churches'.[9] As the century wore on, the teaching of its ministers broadened, but rarely went beyond the boundaries of Evangelical belief. Victorian Con-gregationalists aspired to be thinking Evangelicals.

Baptists were very similar to Congregationalists. The largest section, the Particular Baptists, had retained their Calvinist belief in the redemption of a 'particular' group, the elect. They included manufacturers and shopkeepers in their ranks, perhaps in rather smaller numbers than the Congregationalists, and also drew extensively on the skilled workers. Their local churches were independent, self-governing communities, but they also had regional associations and a national Union, begun in 1812 but reinvigorated in 1832.[10] They differed from the Congregationalists, and from nearly all other Nonconformists, in upholding believer's baptism. The ordinance of baptism should not be administered to uncomprehending infants, they taught, but only to those who were conscious of a personal faith. The majority of Baptists had come to accept that communion should be open to other Christians who had not been baptised as

---

[8] Albert Peel, *These Hundred Years: a history of the Congregational Union of England and Wales, 1831–1931* (London, 1931); R.T. Jones, *Congregationalism in England, 1662–1962* (London, 1962); Clyde Binfield, *So Down to Prayers: studies in English Nonconformity, 1780–1920* (London, 1977).

[9] Robert Vaughan, *Congregationalism* (London, 1842), in John Briggs and Ian Sellers, eds, *Victorian Nonconformity* (London, 1973), p. 103.

[10] E. A. Payne, *The Baptist Union: a short history* (London, 1959).

believers, but traditionalists insisted on the strict policy of making believer's baptism a condition for receiving communion. Feeling ran high, with a copy of a book favouring open communion being burned on a village green near Bury St Edmunds.[11] Many of the traditionalists gradually separated during the Victorian era into a distinct denomination of 'Strict and Particular Baptists', a withdrawn sect nourished by Puritan piety that was strong in East Anglia and the South-East.[12] The main body of Baptists expanded under the impulse of Evangelicalism, especially in parts of the Midlands and South Wales. In the East Midlands another Evangelical group, the New Connexion of General Baptists, had developed a virile witness.[13] They were 'General' because they believed in general redemption, the possibility of any man or woman being saved; they were 'New' because they had split off in 1770 from the old General Baptists who had seventeenth-century origins but who in the nineteenth century were moving at varying speeds towards Unitarianism.[14] In 1851 the various branches of Baptists together possessed 2,789 places of worship and 3.3% of the population. In Charles Haddon Spurgeon they boasted the greatest of Victorian preachers. Partly because of his vigorous influence on church planting, the Baptists main-tained their dynamism more than most other Nonconformists up to the end of the century and beyond.[15]

Another body with origins in the seventeenth century was the Society of Friends, usually known as the Quakers. But the Quakers had always stood apart from the 'Three Denomi-nations' of the Old Dissent—the Presbyterians/Unitarians, Independents and Baptists—because of their own peculiarities. The supreme authority in religion for Quakers was 'the light within', the personal conviction that illuminated the path of duty. Their wor-ship was normally conducted in silence until members, moved, as they believed, by the Spirit of God, led the meeting in prayer,

---

[11] William Cuff, *Fifty Years' Ministry, 1865–1915: memories and musings* (London, 1915), p. 21.

[12] Kenneth Dix, *Strict and Particular: English Strict and Particular Baptists in the Nineteenth Century* (Didcot, 2001).

[13] Frank Rinaldi, *'The Tribe of Dan': a study of the New Connexion of General Baptists, 1770–1891* (Milton Keynes, 2008).

[14] Ian Sellers, 'The Old General Baptists, 1811–1915', *Baptist Quarterly* 24 (1971).

[15] J. H. Y. Briggs, *The English Baptists of the Nineteenth Century* (Didcot, 1994).

reflection or Bible reading. Women could participate alongside men and some, such as Elizabeth Fry, the prison reformer, were among the most respected travelling ministers. Friends held that dress, language and manners should be 'plain', a principle that dictated the wearing of clothes cut to seventeenth-century styles, the archaic use in speech of 'Thou' rather than 'You' and the replacement of the standard names of the months, pagan by origin, with 'First month', 'Second month' and so on. Such practices, reinforced by a tight-knit and centralised structure of business meetings, ensured a powerful sense of solidarity. Any member marrying outside the sect was automatically expelled. Not surprisingly, numbers were declining when, in 1851, it was reported that there were 371 meeting houses attracting only 0.1% of the population. It was recognised in the 1850s that the Society was doomed to extinction unless it changed its ways. From 1860 the distinctive forms of outward witness became optional and the marrying of non-Quakers no longer entailed exclusion. Partly for this reason, numbers recovered from the mid-1860s. The improvement was also because Evangelicalism had permeated the Society so that it organised outreach meetings, Sunday schools and (a Quaker speciality) adult schools. Victorian Quakers were predominantly urban and heavily involved in commerce, banking and manufacturing. The Society of Friends possessed a higher social profile and greater per capita wealth than any other denomination. The influence of the Quakers, like that of the Unitarians, was out of all proportion to their small numbers.[16]

The New Dissent, which dated back only to the eighteenth century, consisted of the various branches of Methodism.[17] It was the largest sector of Nonconformity. In 1851 the Methodist bodies together occupied 11,007 places of worship and served 7.7% of the population. The genius of John Wesley had created in Methodism an efficient harvester of souls and the pen of his

[16] Elizabeth Isichei, *Victorian Quakers* (Oxford, 1970). T. C. Kennedy, *British Quakerism, 1860-1920: the transformation of a religious community* (Oxford, 2001).

[17] It is best to adhere to this, the established usage. A. D. Gilbert applies the term 'New Dissent' to the Congregationalists and Baptists who had been revitalised by the Evangelical Revival (in *Religion and Society in Industrial England* [London, 1976], pp. 36-39), but this practice is confusing. The term 'Evangelical' can be used to distinguish the sections of the Old Dissent that felt an imperative to mission from their predecessors and contemporaries that did not.

brother Charles had provided converts with exuberant hymns to sing. Even at the end of the Victorian period the Methodists were noted among Nonconformists for their enthusiasm. 'The joyful assurance of the favour of God', it was said in 1903, 'is one of the chief marks of a Methodist'.[18] Wesleyan doctrine differed from Calvinism in holding that salvation, though once accepted, could subsequently be lost through lapsing into sin; and that a state of entire holiness could be attained by the believer before death. Both beliefs encouraged Methodists to pay special attention to their religious experience. Week by week they would assemble in classes of eight to a dozen to report on their spiritual progress. It was a sign of the cooling of zeal when, in the last decades of Victoria's reign, it became impossible to induce chapel-goers to attend a class.[19] Laypeople supervised the classes and undertook most of the preaching, but in the organisation founded by Wesley final authority lay with the ministers who attended the annual Conference. The manipulation of power by a small coterie surrounding Jabez Bunting, 'the Methodist pope', aroused huge resentment in the 1840s and led to one of a series of secessions from the Wesleyan Methodist connexion. Yet the great majority of Methodists remained loyal to the original denomination, which in 1851 attracted as many as 5.1% of the population. It was particularly numerous in Cornwall, Lincolnshire and Yorkshire, and was powerful in most industrial areas. The Wesleyan Methodists drew on all social grades, but had more of the well-to-do than most other Nonconformists. As early as 1861 they set up a Fund for Watering Places to cater for the prosperous Wesleyans who sought relaxation in coastal resorts.[20] Wesleyan Methodism was the strongest denomination in Nonconformity.[21]

The seceding bodies nevertheless each contributed something distinctive to the Nonconformist mosaic. The first dissentient body, the Methodist New Connexion, had arisen during the 1790s

---

[18] George Jackson, *The Old Methodism and the New* (London, 1903), p. 43.

[19] H. D. Rack, 'The Decline of the Class-Meeting and the Problem of Church Membership in Nineteenth-Century Wesleyanism', *Proceedings of the Wesley Historical Society* 39 (1973).

[20] H. D. Rack, 'Wesleyan Methodism 1849–1902', in Rupert Davies *et al.*, ed., *A History of the Methodist Church in Great Britain*, 3 (London, 1983), p. 129.

[21] David Hempton, *Methodism: empire of the Spirit* (New Haven, 2005).

in the wake of Wesley's death and the French Revolution, when levelling ideas were abroad and the pretensions of the Methodist Conference had become in-tolerable.[22] The New Connexion asserted the rights of laypeople to participate in church govern-ment and created a more rational, less emotional ethos than the Wesleyans. The New Connexion did not become large, in 1851 serving only 0.3% of the population, but in particular localities, such as Rochdale, it put down deep roots. A tiny body of Independent Methodists with self-governing churches also sprang up in and around Lancashire from the early years of the century; a small group of Tent Methodists specialising in evangelism under canvas arose in the Bristol area.[23] Much stronger, with 1.5% of the population in 1851, was the Primitive Methodist Connexion. It originated around 1810 as a group of revivalists who wanted to use techniques such as all-night camp meetings that were frowned on by the Wesleyan authorities.[24] There were frequent pulses of enormous growth, especially among agricultural labourers, fishermen and miners, and particularly in Yorkshire and the North Midlands.[25] Of all the Non-conformist denominations, the Primitives with their emotional intensity had most appeal to the poor. As late as the 1870s a woman would fall as if dead in one of their meetings or a
minister would stride into a railway compartment to demand of the passengers whether they were converted.[26] A similar but smaller body, the Bible Christians, which in 1851 catered for only 0.2% of the population, was confined almost entirely to Devon and Cornwall and to groups of migrants from those counties.[27] In the north of England and especially round Leeds, there were two secessions from the Wesleyans in protest against Conference

---

[22] D. N. Hempton, *Methodism and Politics in British Society, 1750–1850* (London, 1984), ch. 3.

[23] John Dolan, *The Independent Methodists: a history* (Cambridge, 2005).

[24] J. S. Werner, *The Primitive Methodist Connexion: its background and early history* (Madison, WI, 1984).

[25] E.g. R. W. Ambler, *Ranters, Revivalists and Reformers: Primitive Methodism and rural society: South Lincolnshire, 1817–1875* (Hull, 1989).

[26] J. Stephenson, *The Man of Faith and Fire, or, the life and work of the Rev. G. Warner* (London, 1902), pp. 144, 151.

[27] M. J. L. Wickes, *The Westcountry Preachers: a new history of the Bible Christian Church (1815–1907)* (Hartland, Devon, 1987).

authoritarianism, the Protestant Methodists (1828) and the Wesleyan Methodist Association (1835).[28] Both merged with the bulk of those who left the Wesleyans in a great convulsion during the years 1847–51 to form the United Methodist Free Churches. A small remnant of seceders, chiefly around Sheffield, established the Wesleyan Reform Union (1859),[29] but it was the UMFC that became the third largest branch of Victorian Methodism. In 1851 its constituent groups attracted 0.6% of the population. Ecclesiastically the UMFC stressed the privileges of local churches; politically they had few of the inhibitions of the older bodies about avowing their Liberalism.[30] Their existence was testimony to the staunch opinions that were a symptom of growth in early Victorian Methodism.[31]

Not all who were called Methodists were followers of John Wesley. The Calvinistic Methodists, like the Wesleyans, had sprung up in the eighteenth century, but they did not accept Wesley's theology. They upheld the same Calvinistic teaching as the Old Dissent and so were organised separately from the Wesleyans. In England most of them had disappeared, although a rump survived in Lady Huntingdon's Connexion, drawing 0.2% of the population to worship in 1851 and associating closely with the Independents.[32] In Wales, however, the Calvinistic Methodists flourished and became the largest denomination.[33] As a proportion of the population in England and Wales in 1851 Welsh Calvinistic Methodist attendants were 0.8% but in the principality alone the proportion was as high as 15%. Their evangelistic zeal and their efficient organisation helped their growth, and another key to

---

[28] D. A. Gowland, *Methodist Secessions: the origins of Free Methodism in three Lancashire towns: Manchester, Rochdale, Liverpool* (Manchester, 1979).

[29] *Origin and History of the Wesleyan Reform Union* (Sheffield, 1896).

[30] O. A. Beckerlegge, *The United Methodist Free Churches: a study in freedom* (London, 1957).

[31] Robert Currie, *Methodism Divided: a study in the sociology of ecumenicalism* (London, 1968), ch. 2.

[32] There is no adequate history of the Connexion for after the eighteenth century, but its Victorian ethos is described in John Westbury-Jones, *Figgis of Brighton* (London, 1917), especially pp. 133-39.

[33] John Roberts, *The Calvinistic Methodism of Wales* (Caernarfon, 1934).

success was their use of the Welsh language. The Oxford Movement's Tract 36 claimed in 1834, after cataloguing the heterogeneous range of Dissenting sects, that there existed, 'especially in Wales, Jumpers and Shakers'.[34] The idea was probably pure imagination. Yet the charge does illustrate the truth that on the fringe of Nonconformity there was a range of small groups, orthodox but sectarian, that almost defy listing. In 1851 both the Moravians[35] and the Brethren[36] served 0.1% of the population. Even smaller were the Inghamites,[37] the Sandemanians,[38] the Scotch Baptists,[39] the Catholic Apostolic Church,[40] the Churches of Christ,[41] the Evangelical Union,[42] the Free Church of England,[43] the Peculiar People[44] and the Cokelers.[45] Later in the century there were to arise a number of Holiness denominations of which by far the best known is the Salvation Army.[46] All held the substance of Christian orthodoxy

---

[34] *An Account of Religious Sects at Present existing in England* (1834), no pagination, quoted by G.I.T. Machin, *Politics and the Churches in Great Britain, 1832 to 1868* (Oxford, 1977), p. 83.

[35] J. E. Hutton, *A History of the Moravian Church* (London, 1909).

[36] H. H. Rowdon, *The Origins of the Brethren, 1825–1850* (London, 1967); Tim Grass, *Gathering to his Name: the story of the Open Brethren in Britain and Ireland* (Milton Keynes, 2006).

[37] R. W. Thompson, *Benjamin Ingham and the Inghamites* (Kendal, 1958).

[38] J. T. Hornsby, 'John Glas and his Movement', Edinburgh PhD dissertation (1936).

[39] D. B. Murray, 'The Scotch Baptist Tradition in Great Britain', *Baptist Quarterly* 33 (1989).

[40] P. E. Shaw, *The Catholic Apostolic Church sometimes called Irvingite: a historical study* (Morningside Heights, New York, 1946).

[41] D. M. Thompson, *Let Sects and Parties Fall: a short history of the Association of Churches of Christ in Great Britain and Ireland* (Birmingham, 1980).

[42] Harry Escott, *A History of Scottish Congregationalism* (Glasgow, 1960), ch. 11.

[43] Frank Vaughan, *A History of the Free Church of England otherwise called the Reformed Episcopal Church* (London, 1938).

[44] Mark Sorrell, *The Peculiar People* (Exeter, 1979).

[45] Peter Jerrome, *John Sirgood's Way: the story of the Loxwood Dependants* (Petworth, 1998).

[46] Jack Ford, *In the Steps of John Wesley: the Church of the Nazarene in Britain* (Kansas City, Missouri, 1968); Tom Noble, *Called to be Saints: a centenary history of the Church of the Nazarene in the British Isles, 1906–2006* (Manchester, 2006). Robert Sandall and A. R.

and some—notably the Brethren and the Salvation Army—
expanded rapidly in the later Victorian period. Each might be
classed as Nonconformist, but only the Moravians and
Inghamites, both products of the Evangelical Revival, together
with the Scotch Baptists, the Churches of Christ and the
Evangelical Union, were generally seen as part of Nonconformity
at the time. Despite the immense diversity of Dissent, when
Victorians spoke of Nonconformists they normally thought of
Unitarians, Congregationalists, Baptists, Quakers and Methodists.

The great variety of Nonconformity made for fierce
interdenominational rivalries. Each body knew that it was in a
competitive market for souls and acted accordingly.
Denominations would try to outdo each other in the interminable
quest for recruits, money and eligible chapel sites. There could
even be wrangles within the same denomination as when, in 1882,
the First Cambridge Primitive Methodist Circuit fell out with the
Second Cambridge Primitive Methodist Circuit over ten shillings
collected in the village of Waterbeach.[47] Members of the Old
Dissent, with its traditions of order and learning, generally looked
down on Methodists for their crude zeal. The standard history of
the Dissenters that circulated in the early Victorian years assured
its readers that the lack of education among Wesleyan preachers
'too fully justified the heavy censure which has been passed upon
this communion, as containing a greater sum of ignorance of the
Scriptures than was ever found in any body of protestants since
the reformation'.[48] On occasion Methodists were quite willing to
return insults, resting their case on the dryness and formality of
the Congregationalists and Baptists. The obituarist of a female
member, writing in the *Methodist New Connexion Magazine* for
1850, could not resist the opportunity for polemic against a rival
body. 'Her parents', it recorded, 'attended the Baptist chapel, but,
like too many, they rested in outward ceremonies; for while
honesty and integrity were in their moral character, there were no
evidences of scriptural and saving piety.'[49] The Baptists, that is to

---

Wiggins, *The History of the Salvation Army*, vols 1–4 (London, 1947–
64); Patricia J. Walker, *Pulling the Devil's Kingdom Down: the
Salvation Army in Victorian Britain* (Berkeley, CA, 2001).

[47] Frank Tice, *The History of Methodism in Cambridge* (London,
1966), p. 75.

[48] David Bogue and James Bennett, *History of the Dissenters*, 4
(London, 1812), p. 392.

[49] *Methodist New Connexion Magazine*, December 1850, p. 614.

say, were probably not Christians at all. Rivalry often reached a
high pitch of intensity in Wales, where Baptists claimed to be
unlike other denominations in having been founded by Christ on
the banks of the river Jordan, and distributed tracts offering £100
prizes to anyone producing a Bible verse that vindicated infant
baptism.[50] Loyalty to a particular chapel fostered in turn a
denominational allegiance that gave many Victorians their
primary sense of identity. A man felt himself to be Primitive
Methodist rather than working-class, a Congregationalist rather
than a small shopkeeper. It is no wonder that the denominations
often fell about each other's ears.

Yet sectarian disputes within Nonconformity were moderated
by the existence of an established church from which they all
alike dissented. Generally the Church of England, with all its
appearance of grand pretensions and sinister sacerdotalism, was
the preferred target for their criticisms. A small number of the
more urbane ministers took joint action with likeminded clergy
from the Church of England under the auspices of the Evangelical
Alliance, founded in 1846, but by that date the co-operation that
had been normal in the early years of the century was already
ailing. It was dealt a mortal blow by the denunciation of all things
Anglican in 1862, the bicentenary of the Great Ejection of
ministers from the Church of England in the aftermath of Charles
II's restoration.[51] Thereafter suspicions of Anglicanism as a whole
powerfully reinforced the growing sense of Nonconformist
solidarity. Ministers were already laying aside the old disputes
between Calvinism and Arminianism in order, for example, to
hold regular meetings for fellowship or (as at Grantham in
Lincolnshire in 1856) to establish a joint Religious Reading
Room.[52] There was even co-operation in training for the ministry
at Carmarthen Academy between orthodox Welsh Independents
and Unitarian opponents of orthodoxy.[53] Personal connections
between chapel folk of different communions were multiplying,
whether in the form of the translocal family networks that tied
together the elite of Nonconformity or the bonds of friendship
between man and man who worked together in the same trade.
Interdenominational transfer became a commonplace. A couple

---

[50] T. M. Bassett, *The Welsh Baptists* (Swansea, 1977), pp. 226, 228.

[51] Peel, *These Hundred Years*, p. 240.

[52] Ambler, *Ranters, Revivalists and Reformers*, p. 77.

[53] J. L. Morgan, *Life of Rev. William Morgan* (London, 1886), pp.
109-10.

moved in 1848 from Witham Congregational Church in Essex to the local Primitive Methodists because no denomination seemed 'so plain and quite so willing to stoop so low, as to go out into highways and hedges and compel the poor and needy and outcasts of Society to come into the field of Christ'.[54] But many shifted their allegiance for less exalted reasons. Marriage between members of different congregations compelled a choice of Sunday destination, and employment moves—increasingly frequent happenings—often meant joining a fresh denomination. Transfer was especially likely if there was no nearby chapel of a person's old allegiance. Thus when, in 1870, H. J. Stokes moved from Monmouth to Aberavon and found no English-speaking Congregational church there, he joined the Bible Christians and became a leading light among them.[55] Chapel was chapel, whatever its formal label. As linkages grew, so Nonconformists became increasingly conscious of a shared self-image, and by the 1890s the majority of them were glad to co-operate through newly founded Free Church Councils. During the Victorian era the Free Churches of England and Wales forged a common identity out of enormous diversity.

---

[54] Leonore Davidoff and Catherine Hall, *Family Fortunes: men and women of the English middle class, 1780–1850* (London, 1987), p. 105.

[55] W. J. Mitchell, *Brief Biographical Sketches of Bible Christian Ministers and Laymen*, 1 (Jersey, 1906), p. 236.

CHAPTER 3

Development and Expansion

For the whole of the period Nonconformity was growing. The chapels were ordinarily pulsating with life, drawing in fresh recruits and setting up new daughter congregations. Church planting was by no means always amicable: multiplication was often a result of division. There were schisms over finer points of doctrine or practice, over clashes between strong personalities and, at least on occasion, over industrial tensions. At Barnoldswick in the West Riding of Yorkshire, for example, a Baptist chapel split in 1869 following an unsuccessful and controversial attempt by the minister to provide work for unemployed weavers.[1] Nevertheless the result of such disputes was normally expansion of the chapel-going population. Growth can be gauged in a variety of ways. One adopted by the report on the 1851 religious census, the only official survey of religion undertaken in Britain before the twenty-first century, was to calculate the change in the number of sittings available for worshippers. Between 1841 and 1851, according to the report, Methodist sittings had increased by 40%, Baptist sittings by 28% and Congregational sittings by 25%.[2] Large as these rates of increase were, they were lower than percentages for earlier decades, and undoubtedly reflected a certain falling away in church growth at the opening of the Victorian era. But figures showing accommodation for worshippers probably bear little relation to the numbers of people actually attending. Because the 1851 census that measured attendances was unique, it is impossible to give an accurate national picture of changes in the number of chapel-goers over time. It is possible, however, to analyse the statistics of church membership gathered by the denominations

---

[1] K. G. Jones, 'The Industrial Revolution: effects upon the Baptist community in Barnoldswick and the resulting "split" in the Baptist Church', *Baptist Quarterly* 30 (1983).

[2] D. M. Thompson, *Nonconformity in the Nineteenth Century* (London, 1972), p. 149.

themselves. They reveal a similar pattern for each of the main Nonconformist bodies. Up to about 1840 they had been growing faster than the population; from then until the 1880s their membership was increasing at roughly the same rate as the population; thereafter their expansion fell behind that of the population.[3] Although during the Victorian years Nonconformity was recruiting less rapidly than in the recent past, it was still doing remarkably well until close to the end of the century. Historians have commonly—and with justice—dwelt on the slackening of the pace of growth, but it is equally important to emphasise that fresh members were being attracted in huge numbers during the whole Victorian epoch. Why did chapel folk multiply? A survey of the various features of Nonconformist life will help indicate the reasons.

One is the success of the Nonconformists in evangelising the countryside. It was not only the Methodists who, with their flexible circuits, possessed the means to establish a presence in the villages. In the half-century before Victoria's accession the Independents and Baptists had also devised systems by which travelling lay preachers could blanket rural areas with open-air sermons and gospel literature.[4] Soon new Nonconformist meeting houses sprang up to challenge the monopoly of the parish churches in most country areas, often with conspicuous success. In the south Lindsey district of Lincolnshire, for example, the 1851 census showed that, at the best attended service of the day, the Wesleyans secured larger congregations than the Anglicans in fifty-one out of seventy-eight parishes.[5] Again, in North Wales, another overwhelmingly rural region, 81% of the attendances at a place of worship on census Sunday belonged to the main Nonconformist groups.[6] The achieve-ment was not shared equally between the denominations in any given area, and so there was great variation in the geographical distribution of the various bodies. Evangelists of the Old Dissent had fanned out from their

---

[3] A. D. Gilbert, *Religion and Society in Industrial England* [London, 1976], pp. 30ff, 37ff.

[4] D. W. Lovegrove, *Established Church, Sectarian People: itinerancy and the transformation of English Dissent, 1780–1830* (Cambridge, 1988).

[5] James Obelkevich, *Religion and Rural Society: South Lindsey, 1825–1875* (Oxford, 1976), p. 195.

[6] B. I. Coleman, *The Church of England in the Mid-Nineteenth Century: a social geography* (London, 1980), p. 40.

traditional centres of strength, mainly in the Midlands and East of England and round Bristol, whereas Methodists of all types had concentrated on the areas neglected by both Church and Dissent, primarily in the North but also in pockets like Cornwall.[7] There was also variation in the types of settlement where Nonconformist places of worship were erected, but it has been shown that the distribution followed a marked pattern. Chapels were usually to be found in open parishes with fragmented landownership, but rarely in close parishes where a single squire held most of the land. Squires seldom strayed from the Church of England, and normally refused to provide building sites for potentially troublesome schismatics. Nonconformists had therefore tended to have chapels in places that had escaped from the dominance of the gentry—places that were new, large, on boundaries, scattered in their populations and/or marked by a range of commercial and industrial occupations.[8] In such settlements Nonconformity flourished, though far less in the last quarter of the century as depression set into arable farming and rural depopulation made headway. Chapel-goers were often dis-proportionately represented among the agricultural labourers who emigrated in these years. Nevertheless in 1898 it was reported that only 200 villages in Britain lacked a Nonconformist meeting of some sort.[9] One of the strengths of Nonconformity was its deep roots in the Victorian countryside.

A complementary point is that Nonconformist structures proved sufficiently adaptable to cope with urbanisation. It was once held that the growing towns of Victorian England and Wales proved resistant to all religious influences, and indeed it was shown that, in general, the larger the city, the lower the level of churchgoing in 1851.[10] Subsequent research, however, has demonstrated that variations in church attendance in the towns reflected variations in church attendance in their rural

---

[7] J. D. Gay, *The Geography of Religion in England* (London, 1971).

[8] Alan Everitt, *The Pattern of Rural Dissent: the nineteenth century* (Leicester, 1972).

[9] James Munson, *The Nonconformists: in search of a lost culture* (London, 1991), p. 41.

[10] E. R. Wickham, *Church and People in an Industrial City* (London, 1957); K.S. Inglis, 'Patterns of Religious Worship in 1851', *Journal of Ecclesiastical History* 11 (1960).

hinterlands.[11] Those who moved into towns from the neigh-
bouring countryside tended to maintain their existing religious
practice. Furthermore the problem of the cities was far more acute
for the Church of England, since there its traditional rural props of
custom and deference were knocked away. Nonconformists could
acquire adequate sites and run up cheap buildings much more
easily. Consequently they did well, especially in some of the
fastest growing urban areas: in 1851 at Bradford they achieved a
65% share of the churchgoing population, and in Stoke-on-Trent
the Methodists by themselves secured a clear majority of
attenders.[12] It is true that the chapels made least impact in the nine
largest cities, but even in London in 1902–03 Nonconformist
worshippers out-numbered Anglicans.[13] It is no wonder that the
Congregational leader Robert Vaughan should in 1843 celebrate
the industrial vigour of the great cities as the fruit of 'a pure
Christianity', or that J. H. Wilson, the secretary of the Congregational Home Missionary Society, writing in 1859, should declare
that the strength of the denomination 'unquestionably lies in the
cities and towns of the Kingdom'.[14] Nonconformity seemed the
natural religion of urban England and Wales. Great chapel
buildings such as the imposing brick Gothic Queen's Road
Baptist Church, Coventry, erected in 1882–84 at a cost of nearly
£12,000, consolidated the Nonconformist presence in the centre
of cities of the second rank.[15] In the suburbs that sprawled
outwards in the final decades of the century, the more affluent
Nonconformists felt entirely at home. At Bowdon Downs
Congregational Church, on the southern outskirts of Manchester,
a communion table of cedar wood from Lebanon and olive wood
from the Mount of Olives provided a suitably inspiring focus for

---

[11] D. H. McLeod, 'Class, Community and Region: the religious
geography of nineteenth-century England', in Michael Hill, ed.,
Sociological Yearbook of Religion in Britain, 6 (London, 1973).

[12] Coleman, *Church of England*, p. 41.

[13] Munson, *Nonconformists*, pp. 40, 11.

[14] Robert Vaughan, *The Age of Great Cities* (London, 1843), p. 360;
Albert Peel, *These Hundred Years: a history of the Congregational
Union of England and Wales, 1831–1931* (London, 1931), p. 237.

[15] Clyde Binfield, *Pastors and People: the biography of a Baptist
Church. Queen's Road, Coventry* (Coventry, 1984), p. 67.

the worship of a section of the city's cotton elite.[16] Nonconformity was fostering a new urban—or rather, suburban—civilisation.

If chapel religion flourished in the large towns of the Victorian age, that is because it appealed to the industrial society that was being forged there for the first time in the history of the world. The social composition of the Nonconformist congregations reveals a distinct skew towards industry, among men as well as among masters. In the pre-Victorian years artisans had probably been over-represented in Nonconformity,[17] and, though afterwards their proportion undoubtedly fell, they still formed a significant section of the chapel communities towards the end of the century. In eight out of ten Bradford Nonconformist places of worship in 1881, skilled manual workers constituted the largest social group among the members. No church entirely lacked semi-skilled and unskilled workers, but both these groups were under-represented in relation to population.[18] Although the trades of the artisans varied enormously from place to place, reflecting the employment structure of the neighbourhood, a similar pattern of strong support from skilled workers and weak support from labourers was very general. Artisan involvement could often crowd out the bourgeoisie: in Bradford 61% of the members of Wibsey Congregational Church were working-class, as were 73% at Leeds Road Baptist Church.[19] Nevertheless the tendency over time was upward social mobility, for manual workers wanted their sons to rise into the expanding ranks of the lower middle classes of clerks, shopkeepers and teachers. By the last two decades of the century 35% of Congregational husbands and 24% of Baptist husbands in Bethnal Green were clerical workers.[20] Even among Primitive Methodists, who, like the Baptists, had a slightly lower average class position than the Wesleyans or Congregationalists, the trend towards rising in the social scale was clear. Whereas in the period 1850–70 only 4% of Ashton-un-

---

[16] Clyde Binfield, *So Down to Prayers: studies in English Nonconformity, 1780–1920* (London, 1977), ch. 8, esp. p. 171.

[17] Gilbert, *Religion and Society*, p. 63.

[18] Rosemary E. Chadwick, 'Church and People in Bradford and District, 1880–1914: the Protestant churches in an urban industrial environment', Oxford DPhil dissertation (1986), p. 158.

[19] Chadwick, 'Church and People in Bradford and District', pp. 156-57.

[20] Hugh McLeod, *Class and Religion in the Late Victorian City* (London, 1974), p. 33.

der-Lyne Primitives were lower middle-class, by 1890–1910 the proportion had risen to one quarter or more.[21] Chapel was valued by some precisely because it was a place where diligent young men could catch the eye of an employer and so gain more desirable situations. Although workpeople readily found a place in Nonconformity, it attracted them partly because it could act as a vehicle for embourgeoisement.

Chapel suited many of those in higher stations of life as well. Dissent was normally distasteful to the aristocracy and gentry, though in 1869 there were three Unitarian peers, Earl Lovelace, Earl Zetland (the head of the English Turf) and Lord Belper (the recently ennobled grandson of an early cotton spinner).[22] Professional men also tended to conform to the established church, though north-eastern Methodists, for example, included architects, bankers, a stockbroker and several lawyers.[23] But the upper echelons of Nonconformity were normally merchants or manufacturers, typical entrepreneurs of their age. They liked to carve out an individual path in religion as much as in business, and appreciated the scope for lay initiative in chapel life. It is not surprising that in Lancashire, the county most transformed by industrialisation, as many early Victorian cotton masters were Nonconformists as were Anglicans.[24] They often wielded enormous power over their operatives, perhaps taking pride, like Sir Titus Salt, the Congregational alpaca manufacturer of Saltaire near Bradford, in not insisting on their employees attending their own place of worship—but no doubt looking out for them there.[25] Christopher Fumess, for example, a Hartlepool United Methodist, built up his shipbuilding business from nothing until, shortly before the First World War, he died a millionaire and a peer.[26] Nonconformists shared fully in the retail revolution towards the

---

[21] C. D. Field, 'The Social Structure of English Methodism: eighteenth–twentieth centuries', *British Journal of Sociology* 28 (1977), p. 209.

[22] *English Independent*, 18 November 1869, p. 1145.

[23] G. E. Milburn, *Piety, Profit and Paternalism: Methodists in Business in the North-East of England, c.1760–1920* (Bunbury, Cheshire, 1983), p. 8.

[24] Anthony Howe, *The Cotton Masters, 1830–1860* (Oxford, 1984), p. 62.

[25] Robert Balgarnie, *Sir Titus Salt, Baronet: his life and its lessons* (London, 1877), p. 143.

[26] Milburn, *Piety, Profit and Paternalism*, pp. 30-31.

end of the century, as the names of the Quaker George Cadbury, the Baptist/Congregationalist J. J. Colman and the Primitive Methodist William Hartley bear witness.[27] It was a typical gesture when, around the close of Victoria's reign, Joseph Nasmith, a Manchester textile machinery manufacturer, gave £2,000 towards the building of Moss Side Unitarian Church on condition that the rest of the congregation raised another £2,000.[28] Such men earned the admiration of their co-religionists and poured wealth back into their denominations. They were attracted by the Nonconformist dynamism that they, in turn, helped to sustain.

Men in general were susceptible to the virile, independent image of Nonconformity. A higher proportion of attenders seem to have been male than at Anglican services. In both York in 1901 and the south London borough of Lambeth in the following year men formed virtually half the adult congregations in the chapels, whereas they constituted barely more than a third of those in the parish churches. In both places men actually formed a majority of the adults attending many of the Nonconformist morning services, even though women constituted the majority of the population.[29] There were, of course, exceptions: a Bible Christian local preacher in Cornwall once prepared a sermon on the text, 'My son, give me thine heart', only to find that the congregation consisted solely of five women.[30] Nevertheless since, even at the end of the Victorian years, male support for Nonconformist worship was so strong, it seems likely that men were disproportionately drawn to the chapels throughout the period. Other stray pieces of evidence point in the same direction, such as the finding that in 1881 59% of the adherents of Horton Lane Congregational Church, Bradford, were men. Yet if attention is turned from the penumbra of adherents to the membership at the core of the chapel communities, a very different picture emerges.

---

[27] A. G. Gardiner, *Life of George Cadbury* (London, 1923); H. C. Colman, *Jeremiah James Colman: a memoir* (London, 1905); A. S. Peake, *The Life of Sir William Hartley* (London, 1926).

[28] Ian Sellers, 'Spanning Victoria and Edward: two urban ministries around 1900', *Transactions of the Unitarian Historical Society* 20 (1991), p. 51.

[29] Edward Royle, *Nonconformity in Nineteenth-Century York* (York, 1985), p. 20; Jeffrey Cox, *The English Churches in a Secular Society: Lambeth, 1870–1930* (Oxford, 1982), pp. 26, 288.

[30] W. J. Mitchell, *Brief Biographical Sketches of Bible Christian Ministers and Laymen*, 1 (Jersey, 1906), p. 241.

At the same juncture only 23% of Horton Lane's members were men.[31] The male proportion of York Baptist members in 1862 was 33%; of four Cumbrian Congregational church memberships over long periods, between 32% and 42%; and at Bradford in 1881 of Congregationalists between 19% and 28%, of Baptists between 20% and 36%, of Wesleyans 34%, of Presbyterians 36% and of Quakers 50%.[32] Men were clearly much less likely than women to take the step of formal admission to membership. The higher figures for Presbyterians and Quakers may be partly explained by their being bound respectively by ethnic and sectarian ties, but a class factor was also in operation there and in the other denominations. Middle-class men normally joined as well as their wives; working-class men did not. It has been suggested that whereas the middle classes saw religious allegiance as an expression of the solidarity of the family, there was a tendency for the working classes to regard religion as a dimension of female responsibility.[33] In any case, the result was that involvement in the regular activities of the chapel was disproportionately a female affair.

That is not to say that women were the leaders. Methodism gave them considerable scope, particularly in the cottage meetings that were still in vogue in the early Victorian years. There women could assume matriarchal roles as spiritual mentors,[34] and later women could still hold office as Methodist class leaders. Female preaching, though far from unknown, was on the decline among Victorian Methodists; and the women itinerant preachers of the early Primitive Methodists and Bible Christians had all but disappeared,[35] a casualty of the respectable doctrine of 'separate spheres', according to which women should confine themselves to

---

[31] Chadwick, 'Church and People in Bradford and District', p. 146.

[32] Royle, *Nonconformity in Nineteenth-Century York*, p. 20; John Burgess, *The Lake Counties and Christianity: the religious history of Cumbria, 1780–1920* (Carlisle, 1984), p. 96; Chadwick, 'Church and People in Bradford and District', p. 145.

[33] Chadwick, 'Church and People in Bradford and District', pp. 162-73.

[34] D. M. Valenze, *Prophetic Sons and Daughters: female preaching and popular religion in industrial England* (Princeton, NJ, 1985).

[35] W. F. Swift, 'The Women Itinerant Preachers of Early Methodism', *Proceedings of the Wesley Historical Society* 28 and 29 (1952–53). K. D. Brown, *A Social History of the Nonconformist Ministry in England and Wales, 1800–1930* (Oxford, 1988), p. 17.

the home. Con-gregationalists and Baptists, for the same reason, initially never chose women as deacons to manage chapel affairs even though the practice had been allowed in the previous century.[36] It was a matter for debate in the two denominations whether a woman should be allowed a vote in the Church Meeting.[37] Although female revivalist preachers sometimes found their way into Congregational and Baptist pulpits in the 1860s,[38] women were not accepted as regular ministers among them. It was the Quakers who recognised women as properly accredited ministers, commissioning female members of their leading families to go on continental or transatlantic preaching tours that could take them away from home for years at a time.[39] In the other main denominations female vocations could be worked out only through orders of deaconesses, uniformed ladies looking much like nurses, that were formed around 1890.[40] Yet it was generally appreciated, as *The Baptist Magazine* put it in 1844, that there was 'a special duty of females to promote the advancement of Messiah's reign'.[41] Women, Bible in hand, did most of the district visiting on behalf of the chapels. They went into hospitals, infirmaries, workhouses, asylums and prisons; they cared for the needs of vagrants, navvies, soldiers, sailors and prostitutes. They organised sewing circles to make clothes for the poor and ran bazaars—in the nineteenth century an exclusively female venture—to raise money for missions at home and abroad.[42] In all these activities, and also in the weekly women's meetings that proliferated in the later Victorian years, they found fulfilment.

---

[36] Leonore Davidoff and Catherine Hall, *Family Fortunes: men and women of the English middle class, 1780–1850* (London, 1987), p. 137.

[37] Davidoff and Hall, *Family Fortunes*, pp. 132-33; *Baptist Magazine*, April 1850, pp. 236-39.

[38] Olive Anderson, 'Women Preachers in Mid-Victorian Britain: some reflexions on feminism, popular religion and social change', *Historical Journal* 12 (1969).

[39] Sheila Wright, 'Quakerism and its Implications for Quaker Women: the women itinerant ministers of York Meeting, 1780–1840', in W. J. Sheils and Diana Wood, ed., *Women in the Church* (Oxford, 1990).

[40] D. M. Rose, *Baptist Deaconesses* (London, 1954). Henry Smith, *Ministering Women* (London, 3rd edn, 1923).

[41] *Baptist Magazine*, December 1844, p. 607.

[42] F. K. Prochaska, *Women and Philanthropy in Nineteenth-Century England* (Oxford, 1980); Linda Wilson, *Constrained by Zeal: female spirituality amongst Nonconformists, 1825-1875* (Carlisle, 2000).

Although it was said of a mid-century minister's wife in the Methodist New Connexion that 'conversations on dress she regarded as contemptible littleness',[43] it may be supposed that exactly such staples of female sociability normally drew them together. Chapel was a place where women could enjoy each other's company.

Children likewise made early friendships through chapel life. Although they were usually present through no choice of their own, the gregarious young could find a large number of their age group in the congregations. Between 36% and 43% of attenders at Nonconformist morning services in London in 1902 were children of fifteen years old or younger—about the same proportion as among the Anglicans.[44] Attendance at a Sunday school was even higher, reaching a peak density in about 1885, when an astonishing 19% of the total population was enrolled.[45] In the later Victorian period it is plain that a child who did not spend some years at Sunday school was unusual. By that date the afternoon session was much more popular than the one preceding morning service, partly because secular instruction had normally been given in the morning and that element in the traditional curriculum was largely redundant after the 1870 Education Act.[46] Before the act one of the great attractions of the Sunday schools, and therefore of the places of worship with which they were linked, had been the elementary education in reading, and sometimes in writing, that they had provided. Working-class parents had not been put off by a fear of indoctrination in middle-class values,[47] for they knew many of the teachers as their neighbours and in any case largely shared those values, based as they were on a Christian ethic. Instruction in the day schools promoted by Nonconformists was very similar, being founded on the

---

[43] *Methodist New Connexion Magazine*, September 1850, p. 398.

[44] Richard Mudie-Smith, ed., *The Religious Life of London* (London, 1904), p. 324.

[45] T. W. Laqueur, *Religion and Respectability: Sunday schools and working-class culture, 1780-1850* (New Haven, 1976), p. 246.

[46] P. B. Cliff, *The Rise and Development of the Sunday School Movement in England, 1780–1980* (Nutfield, Surrey, 1986), pp. 168, 201.

[47] Laqueur, *Religion and Respectability*.

Bible, 'the universal text book', as it was put in 1838.[48] 'What we wish for', according to a report to the Wesleyan Conference in the previous year, 'is...an education which may begin in the Infant School and end in Heaven'.[49] In the years immediately afterwards, the Wesleyans, the other major denominations and the Nonconformist-dominated British and Foreign School Society all poured money into school-building, only to realise by the later 1860s that the expanding population made it impossible for the religious bodies to provide sufficient school places without major state involvement. Most Nonconformist day schools except those run by the Wesleyans were transferred to the school boards after 1870. For that reason the substantial contribution of Nonconformity to early Victorian education— though always very much smaller than the Anglican share—has often been obscured. It was another factor that attracted people to chapel.[50]

Education naturally fostered a demand for the printed word in the Nonconformist world. Each of the Methodist bodies imitated John Wesley by maintaining a connexional book room to issue tracts, hymn books, periodicals, official reports and select titles in theology and biography. They were catering for institutions like the Brierley Hill Primitive Methodist Circuit Local Preachers' Library that was flourishing in 1850.[51] Likewise floods of literature poured from presses managed by individuals such as the Primitive Methodist minister George Warner, who during his lifetime produced between thirty and forty thousand books, booklets and pamphlets on the subject of holiness for cheap or free circulation.[52] Even a tiny denomination, the Churches of Christ,

---

[48] By Henry Dunn of the British and Foreign School Society. Richard Brent, *Liberal Anglican Politics: Whiggery, religion and reform, 1830–1841* (Oxford, 1987), p. 245.

[49] Quoted by F. C. Pritchard, 'Education', in Rupert Davies *et al.*, ed., *A History of the Methodist Church in Great Britain*, 3 (London, 1983), pp. 285-86.

[50] Stephen Orchard and J. H. Y. Briggs, ed., *The Sunday School Movement: studies in the growth and decline of Sunday schools* (Milton Keynes, 2007).

[51] *Primitive Methodist Magazine*, May 1850, p. 298.

[52] J. Stephenson, *The Man of Faith and Fire, or, the life and work of the Rev. G. Warner* (London, 1902), p. 276.

published thirteen different periodicals during Victoria's reign.[53] The Baptists in England issued seventy-two between 1837 and 1865.[54] In Wales denominational magazines flourished as nowhere else, doing a great deal to sustain the vigour of the language. In the single county of Carmarthen, it was discovered by an English lawyer investigating Welsh education in 1847, there were five periodicals published monthly. 'They are mostly sectarian', remarked the lawyer disdainfully, 'and not very temperately written.'[55] The same could have been said of *The Christian Witness*, a contemporary English Congregational magazine edited by John Campbell, who contrived to be highly polemical despite his promise in the prospectus that 'no profound and perplexing theological controversy will be admitted'.[56] Campbell at one time contemplated editing a Nonconformist daily newspaper, but he contented himself with producing weeklies, the even more bellicose *British Banner* and *British Standard*. In 1857 *The Christian World* appeared as a weekly with an appeal to Nonconformists at large, attaining by 1880 a circulation of 130,000, and in 1886 it was joined by *The British Weekly*, a newspaper that was to earn fame for its Presbyterian editor, William Robertson Nicoll, as a literary critic and political commentator.[57] Perhaps the most prolific Nonconformist editor was the Wesleyan T. B. Smithies who, from 1851, was responsible for *The Band of Hope Review*, *The British Workman*, *The Children's Friend*, *The Infant's Magazine*, *The Friendly Visitor*, *The Family Friend*, *The Weekly Welcome* and *The Band of Mercy Advocate*, together with the Earlham series of tracts.[58] All this vast output bears testimony to a huge popular appetite for news, opinion and (especially) improving literature. Its

---

[53] D. M. Thompson, *Let Sects and Parties Fall: a short history of the Association of Churches of Christ in Great Britain and Ireland* (Birmingham, 1980), pp. 220-23.

[54] Rosemary Taylor, 'English Baptist Periodicals, 1790–1865', *Baptist Quarterly*, 27 (1977).

[55] *Reports of the Commissioners of Inquiry into the State of Education in Wales* (London, 1848), p. 11 (R. R. W. Lingen).

[56] Peel, *These Hundred Years*, p. 130.

[57] T. H. Darlow, *William Robertson Nicoll: life and letters* (London, 1925).

[58] G. S. Rowe, *T. B. Smithies (Editor of "The British Workman"): a memoir* (London, 1884), pp. 52-55.

widespread dissemination helps explain why Nonconformity was able to draw and to hold its clientele.

Outreach, however, was an even more important reason for Nonconformist growth. Members of all the Evangelical denominations did not wait for people to straggle in through the chapel doors, but went out in order to proclaim the gospel. A careful study of Lancashire Baptists suggests, in fact, that evangelistic zeal, alongside social circumstances, was the chief explanation for their growth. The first circular letter of the local Baptist Association, issued in the year after Victoria's accession, was entitled 'The duty of individual effort for the conversion of souls'. It enumerated the various incentives to evangelism—the love of Christ, the glory of God, solemn anticipation of judgement and similar considerations—before culminating with the scriptural quotation, 'He that winneth souls is wise'. Steady persistence led not to extraordinary results but to a solid net annual gain of twelve members per church in the county.[59] Recruiting outside their ranks was a constant preoccupation of chapels throughout the country. Cottage meetings, tract distributions and soap-box sermons were standard techniques used in what was called 'aggressive work'. From time to time there were innovations such as the portable open-air harmonium, probably first used around 1880 by the inventive Wesleyan evangelist Thomas Champness.[60] Village preachers kept up some of the momentum of the rural evangelism that made such an impact earlier in the century, while Nonconformists carved up the cities into manageable blocs for regular and sustained house-to-house visitation by volunteers. Together with Evangelicals in the Church of England, they sponsored city missions that employed full-time agents to read and explain the Bible from door to door.[61] There was a Baptist Home Missionary Society and a Congregational equivalent that were designed to supply evangelists and resources in localities

---

[59] John Lea, 'The Growth of the Baptist Denomination in Mid-Victorian Lancashire and Cheshire', *Transactions of the Historic Society of Lancashire and Cheshire*, 124 (1972), pp. 134, 131.

[60] Eliza M. Champness, *The Life-Story of Thomas Champness* (London, 1907), p. 193.

[61] D. M. Lewis, *Lighten their Darkness: the Evangelical mission to working-class London, 1828–1860* (Westport, CT, 1986).

where the chapels were weak.[62] In 1840 the Congregational version possessed 120 agents who were said to be proclaiming the gospel to over 60,000 people a year.[63] Other organisations sprang up later on to further the pressing work: the One by One Band, designed to encourage personal evangelism;[64] a fleet of Joyful News Mission Cars to carry the gospel into out-of-the-way places (another of Thomas Champness' ideas);[65] and, a highly significant development of the 1890s, the formation of local Free Church Councils to sponsor missioners and co-ordinate outreach activity by the various chapels within an area.[66] There was much experimenting with fresh methods because the more enthusiastic leaders were never satisfied with the results of the older ways. Nonconformity grew because that was the fixed resolve of many of its members.

Yet the inflow of new converts was by no means even over the years. Growth rates for the Wesleyans show marked fluctuations from year to year, with net losses punctuating the upward trend in every Victorian decade. Peaks and troughs, similar to the pattern of the economic cycle though not coinciding with it, point to the irregularity of growth based on revivalism.[67] Pulses of religious excitement ran through chapel communities from time to time, particularly in Methodism, turning fringe adherents into zealous believers. As time went by, they tended to die out in more sophisticated quarters, but survived in remoter places where folk piety had it own tenacity. In Cornwall, for example, a New Connexion minister recorded that as late as 1882 revivals were still expected, 'but only periodically, as the Cornish folk look at certain seasons for large catches of fish'.[68] It was expected that

---

[62] Richard Carwardine, 'The Evangelist System: Charles Roe, Thomas Pulford and the Baptist Home Missionary Society', *Baptist Quarterly*, 28 (1980).

[63] Peel, *These Hundred Years*, p. 151.

[64] Margaret Hogben, *'One Thing I do': memoir of Thomas Hogben, founder of the 'One by One' Band* (Stockport, 1921).

[65] Josiah Mee, *Thomas Champness as I knew Him* (London, n.d.), pp. 65-66.

[66] E. K. H. Jordan, *Free Church Unity: history of the Free Church Council movement, 1896–1941* (London, 1956), p. 56.

[67] Robert Currie *et al.*, *Churches and Churchgoers: patterns of church growth in the British Isles since 1700* (Oxford, 1977), pp. 38-42.

[68] R. E. Davies *et al.*, ed., *A History of the Methodist Church in Great Britain*, 4 (London, 1988), p. 558 (W. H. Lockley). Cf. David Luker,

after the fire of revival had burned down there would be no new influx of converts for a while. But for some days the atmosphere would be electric. 'Moans & groans, lamentations & strong crying & tears burst on every side', remembered the same minister. 'A young man at my left...fell to his knees & began to hammer the pew with his hand in a violent way... Then swift as a gunshot he rose & darted out of the chapel. In a few minutes he came back, fell on his knees on the sanded floor in front of the little pulpit, shrieked for mercy in a way to alarm sensitive souls. He was soon on his feet again: he had got the blessing...'.[69] Such scenes were repeated at intervals in many parts of Wales, where a major upheaval of this kind was to be felt in 1904–05.[70] Another widespread movement had taken place in 1859, but it, too, was largely confined to the periphery of the British Isles.[71] One of the reasons is evident from the statement of Lancashire Baptists in the following year censuring 'animal excitement, meetings of excessive length, the interruption of business and the order of families'.[72] Respectability and decorum were gradually gaining the upper hand. Nevertheless organised 'revivals' with visiting speakers delivering evangelistic addresses remained a common feature of chapel life down to the end of the century and beyond. The most effective occasions of this kind took place when, in 1873–75, the Americans Dwight L. Moody and Ira D. Sankey toured the land. Their visit to York in 1873, for instance, led to a membership increase of 70% over two years in the Baptist church of the city.[73] Revivalism, whether of the spontaneous or the

---

'Revivalism in Theory and Practice: the case of Cornish Methodism', *Journal of Ecclesiastical History*, 37 (1986).

[69] Davies *et al.*, *Methodist Church*, 4, p. 559.

[70] Richard Carwardine, 'The Welsh Evangelical Community and "Finney's Revival"', *Journal of Ecclesiastical History*, 29 (1978). Noel Gibbard, *Fire on the Altar: a history and evaluation of the 1904-05 revival in Wales* (Bridgend, 2005).

[71] J. E. Orr, *The Second Evangelical Awakening in Britain* (London, 1949), but cf. D. W. Bebbington, *Evangelicalism in Modern Britain: a history from the 1730s to the 1980s* (London, 1989), pp. 116-17.

[72] Lea, 'Baptist Denomination in Mid-Victorian Lancashire and Cheshire', p. 133.

[73] Royle, *Nonconformity in Nineteenth-Century York*, p. 13. Cf. J. F. Findlay, *Dwight L. Moody: American Evangelist, 1837–1899* (Chicago, Ill., 1969), chap. 5; John Coffey, 'Democracy and Popular Religion: Moody and Sankey's mission to Britain, 1873-1875', in E. F. Biagini,

planned variety, added powerful spurts of expansion to the chapels.

Evangelistic work was not confined to Britain but, through the foreign missionary movement, extended to the ends of the earth. In the home of a chapel artisan family there would probably be a missionary magazine on the table and a collecting box on the mantelpiece. A significant proportion of the estimated 9,000 foreign missionaries from the United Kingdom at the end of the century sprang from Nonconformity.[74] The Wesleyan Methodist Missionary Society was central to connexional affairs because its secretaries were the leading permanent officials in the denomination. Although the Baptist Missionary Society and the London Missionary Society, run chiefly by Congregationalists, were supported by less than half the English churches in their respective denominations at mid-century,[75] they elicited sacrificial devotion from many of their donors, often people in very humble circumstances. The Calvinistic Methodists of Wales originally supported the London Missionary Society, but from 1840 conducted their own overseas work with great enthusiasm.[76] There were also specialist missions like the various efforts on behalf of seafarers in foreign ports and the Welsh Baptist Missions to their fellow Celtic speakers in Brittany.[77] It is true that missionary enthusiasm waxed and waned over the years, with high points around 1840 in the wake of the abolition of slavery, immediately after 1857 when David Livingstone, a LMS missionary, made a stirring appeal for Africa, and in the years after his death in 1873.[78] Although the final phase was more marked among Scottish Presbyterians and Evangelical Anglicans

---

ed., *Citizenship and Community: Liberals, radicals and collective identities in the British Isles, 1865-1931* (Cambridge, 1996).

[74] Brian Stanley, *The Bible and the Flag: Protestant missions and British imperialism in the nineteenth and twentieth centuries* (Leicester, 1990), p. 83.

[75] Brian Stanley, 'Home Support for Overseas Missions in Early Victorian England, c.1838–1873', Cambridge PhD dissertation (1979), p. 194.

[76] J. H. Morris, *The History of the Welsh Calvinistic Methodists' Foreign Mission to the End of the Year 1904* (Caernarfon, 1910).

[77] Roald Kverndal, *Seaman's Missions: their origins and early growth* (Pasadena, CA, 1986). T. M. Bassett, *The Welsh Baptists* (Swansea, 1977), pp. 168-71.

[78] Stanley, *Bible and the Flag*, pp. 78-83.

than among Nonconformists, it also saw the rise to prominence of new faith missions that included some of the more theologically conservative chapels in their constituencies. The work of the China Inland Mission, the pioneer among faith missions, inspired the Bible Christians to launch a venture into China.[79] There were two major consequences for Nonconformists of involvement in overseas work. One was a broadening of horizons to embrace the world—or at least the parts where their missionaries had opened up fields. Their global vision strengthened, for instance, the sense of rivalry with the Roman Catholic Church that was already prompted, especially among the Wesleyans, by evangelism in Ireland.[80] A second consequence was what contemporaries called the reflex effect of missions. News of the triumphs of the gospel overseas induced greater devotion to missionary work at home, and, occasionally, to the conversion of individuals in the chapels themselves.[81] Although overseas enterprise swallowed up a great deal of money, it was probably repaid with interest in terms of church growth.

Victorian Nonconformists rarely lost sight of the principle that human beings have bodies as well as souls. Although the cry that temporal matters such as relief of the poor are less important than the spread of the gospel was sometimes heard, it was quickly met with the reply that philanthropy is equally a Christian obligation.[82] Hence the chapels busied themselves with various forms of social concern. Even a small community like the Baptist church at Southwell, Nottinghamshire, had seven elderly people on its pension list in 1841, and in 1884 a larger city cause like the Derby Road Baptist Church in Nottingham kept 208 blankets for circulation among the needy.[83] In times of distress these were co-ordinated charitable efforts: during the Cotton Famine of 1862–63 the Lancashire Baptist Relief Fund raised and distributed the large sum of nearly £7,000.[84] Individuals might be noted, as was a

---

[79] N. A. Birtwhistle, 'Methodist Missions', in Davies *et al.*, ed., *Methodist Church*, 3, p. 81.

[80] D. N. Hempton, *Methodism and Politics in British Society, 1750–1850* (London, 1984), chap. 5.

[81] Stanley, 'Home Support', pp. 146-51.

[82] E.g., *Baptist Magazine*, August 1842, p. 439.

[83] F. M. W. Harrison, 'The Nottinghamshire Baptists and Social Conditions', *Baptist Quarterly*, 27 (1978), p. 222.

[84] Lea, 'Baptist Denomination in Mid-Victorian Lancashire and Cheshire', pp. 142-43.

Leeds Protestant Methodist, for their humble sick visiting, or else, like an ex-butcher and Baptist minister in the East End of London, for more spectacular feats—in his case, for cutting up nearly two tons of beef for distribution to needy families at Christmas.[85] Some of the boldest initiatives were undertaken by Quakers, whose money underwrote a variety of semi-philanthropic schemes including, at the end of the century, George Cadbury's garden suburb at Bournville near Birmingham, or by Unitarians such as Mary Carpenter, who took up successively the causes of Ragged Schools for destitute children, juvenile delinquents, convicts, girls' education and female suffrage—and the list is not exhaustive.[86] The Congregational minister Andrew Reed championed the cause of mentally handicapped children, founding the unfortunately named Asylum for Idiots, the great Baptist preacher C. H. Spurgeon established an orphanage and the Wesleyan minister T. B. Stephenson launched a children's home.[87] Each spring the Exeter Hall in the Strand rang to stirring appeals on behalf of such worthy causes as the voluntary societies held their 'May Meetings', some of them wholly Anglican but most of them interdenominational. Already at the opening of the period it was noted that there had been a crucial shift in the use of leisure time by Nonconformists, from 'private religious exercises' to 'the service of our benevolent institutions'.[88] Throughout the Victorian years the chapels and the organisations they supported were hives of philanthropic activity. It is no wonder that some of the beneficiaries, whether householders receiving Christmas bounty or orphans rescued from the streets, found their way into chapel pews.

Charitable work, like most other aspects of chapel life, was disproportionately in the hands of the ministers. Some of the more sectarian bodies—chiefly the Quakers, the Churches of Christ and the Brethren—rejected the whole idea of religious professionals,

---

[85] *United Methodist Free Church Magazine*, July 1858, p. 376 (Abraham Holt). Munson, *Nonconformists*, p. 56 (William Cuff).

[86] Gardiner, *George Cadbury*, chap. 9. J. C. Carpenter, *The Life and Work of Mary Carpenter* (London, 1881).

[87] Andrew Reed and Charles Reed, *Memoirs of the Life and Philanthropic Labours of Andrew Reed, D.D.* (London, 1863), ch. 11. Ian Shaw, 'Charles Spurgeon and the Stockwell Orphange: a forgotten enterprise', *Christian Graduate*, September 1976. A. A. Jacka, *The Story of the National Children's Home* (London, 1969).

[88] *Annual Session of the Baptist Union*, p. 28.

but the great majority of Nonconformists believed in a separated ministry. Denominational structures were dominated by ministers: laypeople were entirely excluded from the Wesleyan Conference, the connexional governing body, until as late as 1877, when unordained representatives were grudgingly admitted to one of two consecutive sessions.[89] The great names in the ministry gained enormous respect and influence. George Osborn, who controlled the Wesleyan bureaucracy in the 1870s and 1880s almost as tightly as Jabez Bunting had done earlier in the century, achieved his mastery by a combination of conspicuous debating skills and total connexional loyalty.[90] R. W. Dale, minister of Carr's Lane Congregational Church, Birmingham, was immensely versatile, turning his hand to Liberal politics as readily as to denominational strategy, while at the same time producing theological and devotional works of a high order.[91] In stark contrast with the eminence and fulfilment of such men, however, was the unenviable lot of the ordinary working minister. So pressurised by pastoral responsibilities were most of them that they had no time for outside activities, whether denominational administration, public affairs or publication. Since the average annual salary of an English Baptist minister in 1873 was only about £75, the equivalent of a semi-skilled factory worker's wages, and since a few enjoyed over £500 a year, some must have lived in abject poverty.[92] The demands of the job and low pay ensured a high drop-out rate from the ministry and the frequent clashes with lay leaders in the chapels that led, especially in Methodism, to the creation of so many splinter groups.[93] Yet the educational standard of the ministry was steadily improving as the century wore on, and individuals continued to give of their time unstintingly. A Unitarian commented in 1874 that 'by the culture and faithfulness of ministers, more than any other cause, has

---

[89] Robert Currie, *Methodism Divided: a study in the sociology of ecumenicalism* (London, 1968), p. 160.

[90] George Penman, *I Remember* (London, 1916), pp. 15-24.

[91] A. W. W. Dale, *The Life of R. W. Dale of Birmingham* (London, 1898). J. M. Gordon, *Evangelical Spirituality* (London, 1991), ch. 6.

[92] Brown, *Nonconformist Ministry*, pp. 220, 157.

[93] John Kent, 'The Doctrine of the Ministry in Early Nineteenth-Century Methodism', *The Age of Disunity* (London, 1966). Gowland, *Methodist Secessions*.

Nonconformity been perpetuated'.[94] A Methodist might have been more inclined to couple the ministers with the lay preachers, who among Wesleyans in 1883 outnumbered the ministers by seven to one,[95] but the principle remains valid. The prosperity of the chapels owed a huge debt to the exertions, often in trying circumstances, of the local leaders.

The chief function of the Nonconformist minister, by common consent, was preaching. The most eminent preacher of the Victorian age was C. H. Spurgeon, who rose between 1854 and 1861 from an obscure Baptist pastorate in the Cambridgeshire Fens to the pulpit of the mighty Metropolitan Tabernacle in south London, purpose-built for him and holding nearly 6,000. Always willing to pepper his sermons with wit and to seize any opportunity for publicity, he once preached at Epsom races on the text 'So run that ye may obtain'.[96] The Congregational minister of London's City Temple, Joseph Parker, who was inclined to be jealous of Spurgeon's popularity, often chose to make an impact by springing surprises on his hearers. In 1898, when the Sultan of Turkey held an unsavoury reputation as a persecutor of Christians, Parker denounced him as no friend of the Almighty. 'In the name of God', he went on, 'and speaking of the Sultan, not merely as a man, but as the Great Assassin, I say "God damn the Sultan!"'[97] An astonished congregation briefly held its breath before breaking out in rapturous applause. A sermon by John Rattenbury, a prominent Wesleyan minister who specialised (like Spurgeon) in expositions of the Bible rather than (like Parker) in topical addresses, could be greeted by tears and 'loudest bursts of pent-up feeling'.[98] Welsh preachers often aspired to create an emotional atmosphere in which they were carried along with torrents of eloquence and the congregation's excitement became audible as *hwyl*. Nowhere was preaching more appreciated than in Wales, where at a single gathering of a Baptist association in 1843 there were forty-three sermons,[99] but in England, too, they

---

[94] *Inquirer*, 12 December 1874 (Thomas Hunter), quoted by Brown, *Nonconformist Ministry*, p. 10.

[95] Brown, *Nonconformist Ministry*, p. 143.

[96] Horton Davies, *Worship and Theology in England: from Newman to Martineau, 1850–1900* (Princeton, NJ, 1962), p. 289.

[97] Munson, *Nonconformists*, p. 102.

[98] H. O. Rattenbury, ed., *The Rev. John Rattenbury: memorials* (London, 1884), p. 45.

[99] Bassett, *Welsh Baptists*, p. 272.

were probably the most popular form of reading at mid-century. Subsequent trends in preaching style helped to sustain the appeal of the sermon, though not at the same level. There was a tendency to reduce the number of points, to include less formal argument and to prune away the lush rhetoric that around 1850 was in vogue in the more prosperous congregations. The businesslike preaching of the American revivalist D. L. Moody in 1873–75 accelerated the process, leading to a decline in what one Methodist censured as 'Pretty-ism'.[100] Congregations continued to tolerate sermons of immense length. A survey in 1896 discovered that while the shortest sermon reported on a particular Sunday, by a Primitive Methodist minister at Clitheroe in Lancashire, lasted only five and three quarter minutes, the longest, by a Methodist New Connexion lay preacher, went on for no less than one hour twenty-eight minutes. The normal Nonconformist sermon was about half an hour long.[101] It was an indication that, even at the end of the Victorian era, there was still an appetite for the preacher's words. The sermon was a form of popular entertainment and Nonconformity was happy to oblige.

Relatively little is known about the setting of preaching, the service of worship, partly because chapel-goers did not trouble to record the familiar weekly pattern. An American visitor, however, noticed in the early 1840s that, by contrast with the churches of his homeland, London congregations of several denominations were quiet and restrained. Dissenters bowed in prayer for a minute or two on entering their pews, kept silence after the benediction for about half a minute before leaving, and in between listened to sermons of only moderate worth 'without any indications of restlessness or contempt'.[102] The peak of decorum in Nonconformity was probably to be found in certain south coast congregations of the Countess of Huntingdon's Connexion where, with minor modifications, the liturgy of the Book of Common Prayer was followed.[103] There was also a tendency for the wealthiest congregations of the other denominations to imitate the worship of the Church of England, which in the post-Tractarian era was setting the pace in matters of taste. By 1869 one Congregational church had a communion table emblazoned with the sacred monogram 'IHS', two reading desks, a gowned

---

[100] Mee, *Champness*, p. 45.

[101] *British Weekly*, 19 March 1896, pp. 355-56.

[102] *Baptist Magazine*, July 1842, p. 351.

[103] John Westbury-Jones, *Figgis of Brighton* (London, 1917), p. 81.

minister, repetition of the Lord's Prayer and the *Te Deum* and even 'two crimson velvet bags' for the offering.[104] But it is significant that these arrangements were being reported in a Baptist newspaper in order to be criticised. Like choir anthems then and later, such developments were looked at askance by many Nonconformists as introducing formality where there should be spontaneity. Far more typical of Nonconformist worship was full-throated singing of the hymns of Charles Wesley and Isaac Watts. Even a sophisticated city-centre Baptist church minuted in 1900 that 'praise *should be as congregational as possible*'.[105] Evening gospel services, which were better attended among Victorian Nonconformists than morning worship, tended to be more relaxed so that strangers should feel at home. In rural Methodism informality often shaded into disorder. A good service was one where sinners fell to the floor in anguish or cries of 'Hallelujah!' rent the air. The quarterly love feasts where members delivered their testimonies were far more popular than the rare occasions of communion. Chapel and Sunday school anniversaries, opportunities for showing off new clothes and enjoying the festival atmosphere, were the most thronged of all.[106] Unabashed celebration, a chance of participation, the total absence of priestcraft—these were the hallmarks of many Nonconformist services. Although there were styles of worship to cater for the sophisticated preferences of the more select suburbs, there were many other chapels in town and countryside where unpretentious folk felt at home.

There was similar variety in the architectural expression of Nonconformity. On the one hand, there was a range of recent utilitarian brick buildings, of older cramped meeting houses up picturesque back lanes and (from the 1870s) of movable tin tabernacles. Many were scarcely superior to the cottages and barns where Nonconformists had gathered before they possessed their own places of worship. A typical Primitive Methodist chapel in a Durham mining community, according to the connexion's own magazine in 1896, was 'a plain, unpretentious building, commodious enough, but lacking both in beauty and comfort'.[107] Yet round such humble structures there grew up powerful

---

[104] *Freeman*, 16 April 1869, p. 302.

[105] Binfield, *Pastors and People*, p. 107.

[106] Obelkevich, *Religion and Rural Society*, pp. 224-30.

[107] *Primitive Methodist Magazine*, 1896, p. 830, in John Briggs and Ian Sellers, eds, *Victorian Nonconformity* (London, 1973), p. 35.

affections, as the Methodist authorities were to discover in the
twentieth century when they tried to close those deemed
superfluous. In the early Victorian period they also enjoyed a
crucial advantage over the parish churches in being warmed by a
stove in winter. Only from about 1860 onwards did the Anglicans
introduce heating.[108] On the other hand, rising Nonconformists
craved more aesthetic settings for worship, what a critic in 1858
called 'genteeler roads to heaven'.[109] In the early years of the
reign the classical style had the edge, producing buildings like the
Congregational chapel in Angel Street, Worcester, with its many-
columned portico, that is illustrated on the frontispiece of this
book. The rival Gothic style, though it was denounced by some as
'Romish-Priest-architecture',[110] steadily made headway until by
the 1890s it was the expected medium. In that decade, for
instance, there rose the new Albion Congregational Church,
Ashton-under-Lyne, boasting Perpendicular architecture and
stained glass windows to Burne-Jones designs that portrayed
assorted saints, graces and virtues.[111] All this display was not
straightforward imitation of the Church of England, even if
emulation played a large part, for Gothic was adapted to
Nonconformist needs.[112] Thus in 1850 the Wesleyan minister and
architect F. J. Jobson insisted that the Gothic style could be
modified by providing classrooms, vestries, seats for children and
scope for enlargement. Thus it would be a worthy replacement for
the existing chapels in industrial cities that were 'more like
warehouses or factories than Houses of God'.[113] The newer, more
tasteful buildings were appreciated by those who had been
educated to revere the artistic theories of John Ruskin, but the
older, simpler styles still satisfied the man or woman in the street.

---

[108] Obelkevich, *Religion and Rural Society*, p. 110.

[109] *Freeman*, 17 November 1858, p. 702.

[110] *Baptist Magazine*, March 1867, pp. 171-72.

[111] Clyde Binfield, '"We Claim our Part in the Great Inheritance": the
message of four Congregational buildings', in Keith Robbins, ed.,
*Protestant Evangelicalism: Britain, Ireland, Germany and America,
c.1750–c.1950: essays in honour of W. R. Ward* (Oxford, 1990), p. 218.

[112] Binfield, *So Down to Prayers*, p. 146.

[113] F. J. Jobson, *Chapel & School Architecture as Appropriate to the
Buildings of Nonconformists, particularly to those of the Wesleyan
Methodists* (London, 1850), in Davies *et al.*, ed., *Methodist Church*, 4,
p. 492.

The very diversity of its architecture contributed to Nonconformity's breadth of appeal.

The expansion of the chapel communities during Victoria's reign, then, may be explained in terms of a large number of factors. It has been suggested by Robert Currie and others that among the reasons for church growth, environmental factors are chief. Although the recruitment policies of denominations play a part, they argue, circumstances beyond ecclesiastical control are more important. External factors such as economic conditions, political crises and war affect the size of the social reservoir from which churches draw their new members, and when the reservoir runs dry so does the flow of recruits. Thus in the case of Nonconformity, its natural constituency consisted predominantly of skilled manual workers. As their proportion in the population fell after 1840, so the expansion of the chapel community slowed down.[114] What is to be made of this theory? It is undoubtedly true that artisans were found disproportionately in chapel. Furthermore the conditions of the early industrial epoch were especially favourable to the spread of Evangelical religion outside the established church. The breakdown of rural dependency on the gentry made for independent thinking, and the rigidity of Anglican structures gave Nonconformity an early advantage in urban areas. Later on, with the expansion of the service sector in the late Victorian economy, the number of lower middle-class jobs increased, and the chapels, with their facilities for training and lay leadership, were well placed to fill the new vacancies from their ranks. Circumstances—and a rather broader range of circumstances than Currie and his co-authors allow—therefore favoured chapel growth during the nineteenth century. But without its internal strengths, Nonconformity could not have capitalised on the advantages it enjoyed. Its ministers, lay activists and generous donors showed wisdom as well as dedication in providing facilities for children, opportunities for women and help for the needy. They were willing to adapt their worship and their architecture to cater for rising social groups. Above all, they made outreach a priority: regular evangelism supplemented by revivalism, overseas missions and a vast output of literature ensured that congregations increased. It is the exception that proves the rule. Despite an initial strength among artisans and despite a heavy involvement in philanthropy, the Unitarians, who

---

[114] Currie *et al.*, *Churches and Churchgoers*, pp. 37, 96-99, 56-57.

rarely went in for outreach, remained a small body by comparison
with the Evangelical Nonconformists or even (in relation to its
size) a fringe group such as the Mormons.[115] In the last resort it
was an energetic and flexible strategy of mission that made
Victorian Nonconformity grow.

---

[115] R. O. Owen, 'Church Growth in England, 1841–1914', in V. B.
Bloxham *et al.*, ed., *Truth will Prevail: the rise of The Church of Jesus
Christ of Latter-Day saints in the British Isles, 1837–1987* (Solihull,
1987), p. 199.

CHAPTER 4

The Helmstadter Thesis

Perhaps the most stimulating academic debate relating to Nonconformity in Victoria's reign is the contention of R. J. Helmstadter that the chapels passed through an epoch of confident individualism lasting from the 1830s to the 1880s before turning at the end of the century towards new attitudes that undermined their optimism and even their viability. The essay setting out this argument was republished in volume 4 of the Open University series *Religion in Victorian Britain* — and rebutted by the editor in volume 1.[1] Helmstadter holds that in Nonconformity's Victorian heyday, religious, social and political convictions were mutually reinforcing since they all posited the primacy of the individual conscience. The prevailing religious opinions were Evangelical, insisting that a person must personally undergo the crisis of conversion in order to enter a life of faith. The predominant social views, those of the businessmen who shaped Nonconformist life, laid stress on individual effort as the remedy for poverty and the key to progress. In politics the chapels championed the freedom of the individual and their own members' right to obey conscience without penalty. The synthesis of these attitudes crumbled when, in the 1880s, it was challenged by biblical criticism, the social gospel and collectivism in politics. The juncture when the phrase 'the Nonconformist conscience' was coined to describe the sense of public responsibility in the Free Churches, the year 1890, was paradoxically the point when the exaltation of the individual conscience had just fallen into decay. Helmstadter's main contentions form an attractive hypothesis that draws together many of the threads in Nonconformist life, par-

---

[1] R.J. Helmstadter, 'The Nonconformist Conscience', in Peter Marsh, ed., *The Conscience of the Victorian State* (Hassocks, Sussex, 1979), reprinted in Gerald Parsons, ed., *Religion in Victorian Britain*, 4 (Manchester, 1988). Gerald Parsons, 'From Dissenters to Free Churchmen: the transitions of Victorian Nonconformity', in Parsons, ed., *Religion in Victorian Britain*, 1 (Manchester, 1988).

ticularly in the area of public affairs. Explicit evidence in its support is not hard to find. There is, for example, a verdict delivered in 1894 on Henry Allon, possibly the most cultured Congregational minister of his time, who had died in his seventies two years earlier. 'In political and social matters', wrote Allon's biographer, 'he was a strong Individualist, and never quite understood the newer tendencies of to-day. His emphasis was upon individual enterprise and character rather than collective action...'.[2] Because Allon had been moulded by the heroic age beginning in the 1830s, Helmstadter would conclude, he was ill at ease in the period opening in the 1880s. So it is worthwhile evaluating the Helmstadter thesis. Since the trends at the end of Victoria's reign will be dealt with in the last chapter of this book, attention here will concentrate on the epoch between the 1830s and the 1880s, Helmstadter's golden years of individualism; and since it has already been shown that there was indeed an individualistic strain in the Evangelical scheme of salvation, the assessment can focus mainly on Nonconformist social and political attitudes during that time.

Self-help was the kernel of chapel social theory. Edward Baines, the Congregational editor of *The Leeds Mercury*, set six points of his own against the demands of the Chartists: Education, Religion, Virtue, Industry, Sobriety, Frugality.[3] It was a recipe for a self-made man, the formula that had brought prosperity to the industrial north. The desirable qualities are specified more fully in the chapter titles of a biography of a Wesleyan merchant, Walter Powell, that was designed to excite emulation: singleness of purpose, and regard for the will of God; conscientious shrewdness, astuteness, firmness, energy and push; business talent, laboriousness, concentration; conscientious intelligence, foresight, insight, promptitude and regularity; prudence, caution, judiciousness and vigilance; frugality, fairness and contentment; moderation.[4] The paragon possessed of all these attributes was bound to prosper—so long as there was a minimum of interference by government in commercial dealings. Hence Nonconformist spokesmen such as the Quaker John Bright stoutly

---

[2] W. H. Harwood, *Henry Allon, D.D.: pastor and teacher* (London, 1894), p. 106.

[3] Clyde Binfield, *So Down to Prayers: studies in English Nonconformity, 1780–1920* (London, 1977), p. 79.

[4] Benjamin Gregory, *The Thorough Business Man: memoirs of Walter Powell*, 7th edn (London, 1880), pp. vii-viii.

resisted the efforts of the future Lord Shaftesbury and his fellow Evangelical Anglican campaigners to impose tight statutory limits on the hours that could be worked in factories. Hence, too, the Anti-Corn Law League, in which Bright took a leading part, demanded the repeal of legislation restricting freedom of trade.[5] *The Nonconformist* newspaper, in fact, envisaged a rolling back of the state in every department of life, a view set out in 1847 in an essay on 'The Province of Civil Government'. 'It is neither chief baker', declared the article, 'nor butler, nor purveyor, nor almoner, nor presiding pedagogue, nor high priest—but it is SWORD-BEARER, and all that such an office properly implies— nothing more, and nothing less.'[6] Thus education, as Edward Baines insisted, was to be a field for voluntary effort, not for state action.[7] The schools, according to the Nonconformist vanguard in the middle years of the century, must be free of government involvement so as to inculcate the values of true religion. If the state confined itself to sword-bearing, that is to basic defence and the maintenance of public order, it would be able to impose a far lighter burden on the tax-payer. In 1854 a writer in *The General Baptist Magazine* longed for an end to 'the oppressive weight of taxes that grind nations to the dust'.[8] The mainstream of Nonconformist opinion wanted an approximation to laissez-faire so that individuals might be at liberty to forge their own future. A social theory so supportive of personal enterprise and so suspicious of the state is clear evidence in favour of the Helmstadter thesis.

There is more supporting evidence from the distinctive causes of their own the Nonconformists championed. Less than a decade before Victoria came to the throne, they had all been formally second-class subjects of the crown. Legislation from the seventeenth century, the Test and Corporation Acts, had excluded them from sitting on town councils, and, although the statutes were largely a dead letter, there was technically a risk that they would be invoked against Dissenters once again. Only in 1828 were the obnoxious acts repealed.[9] With the passing of the Reform Act in 1832, Dissenters wished to consolidate their new political

---

[5] Keith Robbins, *John Bright* (London, 1979), pp. 18-19, 31-64.

[6] *The Nonconformist* quoted by *Baptist Magazine*, October 1847, p. 633.

[7] Binfield, *So Down to Prayers*, pp. 80-91.

[8] *General Baptist Magazine*, July 1854, p. 308.

[9] D. W. Bebbington in *Baptist Quarterly*, 27 (1978), p. 376.

standing. Why should their remaining grievances not be swept away? From the 1830s onwards there was a campaign of gathering force to eliminate the five main Dissenting disabilities. The only statutory records of birth were the baptismal registers of the Church of England, a particular problem for Quakers and Baptists who repudiated infant baptism altogether. All marriages except those of Jews and Quakers had to take place in a parish church, and, though Nonconformists in general conformed to the practice, there was special resentment amongst Unitarians who were compelled to use a liturgy designed for believers in the Trinity. Burials in parish churchyards, often the only available places of interment, also had to observe the Book of Common Prayer. Nonconformists could not enter the University of Oxford or graduate from Cambridge, effectively handicapping them in the competition for many professional posts. And, most serious of all, rates for the upkeep of the fabric of the parish church were levied on all inhabitants, whether or not they were Anglicans, unless opponents could muster a majority at the annual vestry meeting that fixed the rate.[10] The church rate grievance hit the pocket of the Nonconformists, but it was its symbolic quality that irritated them far more. It was not a question of money, declared *The Baptist Magazine* in 1865, but 'a question of caste and domination'.[11] The privileges of the Church of England seemed tools of the traditional landed interest for keeping Dissenters down. It is hardly surprising that a growing number, especially from the small towns in the South and Midlands where there was awareness of continuing rural discrimination, took the further step of demanding disestablishment.[12] The Church of England should be divorced entirely from the state. Although Nonconformists created in the Liberation Society a powerful pressure group to assert their claims, it is clear that concessions were made to them only when it suited Whig or Liberal governments.[13] By 1880, however, when Gladstone's second administration eliminated the

---

[10] Owen Chadwick, *The Victorian Church*, 1, 2nd edn (London, 1970), pp. 79-89.

[11] *Baptist Magazine*, April 1865, p. 239.

[12] D. M. Thompson, 'The Liberation Society, 1844–1868', in Patricia Hollis, ed., *Pressure from Without in Early Victorian England* (London, 1974), pp. 229-30.

[13] Olive Anderson, 'Gladstone's Abolition of Compulsory Church Rates: a minor political myth and its historiographical career', *Journal of Ecclesiastical History*, 25 (1974).

burials grievance, all the major disabilities had been abolished. The era between the 1830s and 1880 therefore has a character of its own in the annals of political Nonconformity. It was a time when, as Helmstadter contends, Dissent was mobilised to assert the right of the individual conscience to be treated with respect.

Yet the argument about the prevalence of individualism can be taken much too far, for it neglects several deeply rooted features of Nonconformist life. For one thing, it ignores the centrality of the family in chapel affairs. By the 1830s the domestic ideology that allocated roles according to gender—the public affairs of business and politics for men, the private affairs of household and charity for women—had become so deeply embedded in the national consciousness that religious arguments in its favour were no longer necessary. Although women continued to play a major, if hidden, part in family businesses, they were expected, for the sake of their own standing in the world, to concentrate on the domestic arts.[14] Thus the deceased wife of a Methodist New Connexion minister was praised for her skills about the house. 'Cleanliness with her,' wrote the proud widower, 'amounted almost to idolatry.'[15] The division of labour within the household meant that prosperity was designed as much to guarantee leisure for the wife and daughter as to further the husband's career or to set up the sons in business. The welfare of the family was the primary aim in life. Often the extended family within a chapel community could be substantial: between 1820 and 1890 Charlotte Baines, mother of Edward, was followed in membership at Salem Congregational Church, Leeds, by seven children, seven children-in-law, twenty grandchildren, seven grandchildren-in-law, two great grandchildren and four step-great-grandchildren.[16] With a high proportion of this army of relations on parade each Sunday, family obligations could hardly be forgotten. Business enterprise, furthermore, was not a matter of unbridled acquisition. Christian teaching on the duty of generosity with money was heard regularly from the pulpit, and from 1860 there was even a

---

[14] Leonore Davidoff and Catherine Hall, *Family Fortunes: men and women of the English middle class, 1780–1850* (London, 1987), chs 3 and 5.

[15] *Methodist New Connexion Magazine*, September 1850, p. 398.

[16] Binfield, *So Down to Prayers*, pp. 72-73.

Systematic Beneficence Society to encourage regular giving.[17]
Hence the Non-conformist manufacturer recognised
responsibilities to a wider circle than his family—to his
congregation, to his town and especially to his workforce. Some
devised elaborate schemes for their employees' welfare: Sir Titus
Salt, for instance, created a model village under the lee of his
alpaca mill, leading his workpeople to reciprocate by presenting
him with 'a colossal bust of himself' at a grand feast in the
grounds.[18] Intense loyalty of operatives to their master seems to
have been the norm.[19] The values of chapel members—of the
dominant figures as well as the rank and file—were moulded by
their family responsibilities and their obligations at work. Their
out-look on the world, rather than being narrowly individualistic,
was coloured by a powerful communal sense.

Large-scale industrial and political movements associated with
the chapels were also shot through with the spirit of mutuality.
Nonconformity, as a critic of Helmstadter's case has pointed out,
was a seed-bed for trade unionism even before 1880, particularly
in agriculture and the mining industry.[20] Workers combined to
demand a just appreciation of their efforts in pay, security and
conditions. Although most pro-minent Nonconformists, ministers
and laymen alike, deprecated union formation as an attempt to
interfere with the operation of free contract, a number, such as T.
D. Mathias, minister of Bethel Baptist Chapel, Merthyr Tydfil,
gave outspoken support even to strike action.[21] In the 'Revolt of
the Field', the wave of agricultural trade unionism beginning in
1872, over half the local union leaders in Lincolnshire and
Norfolk and nearly half in Suffolk were Methodists. Working-
class solidarity came naturally to men whose speeches were
suffused with biblical imagery about Moses leading the people of

---

[17] Jane Garnett, '"Gold and the Gospel": systematic beneficence in
nineteenth-century England', in W.J. Sheils and Diana Wood, ed., *The
Church and Wealth* (Oxford, 1987).

[18] Robert Balgarnie, *Sir Titus Salt, Baronet: his life and its lessons*
(London, 1877), pp. 158-68.

[19] Patrick Joyce, *Work, Society and Politics: the culture of the factory
in late Victorian England* (London, 1980).

[20] Parsons, 'From Dissenters to Free Churchmen', pp. 95-96.

[21] Aled Jones and John Saville, 'Thomas Davies Matthias (1823–
1904)', in J. M. Bellamy and John Saville, ed., *The Dictionary of
Labour Biography*, 7 (London, 1984), pp. 178-82.

Israel to deliverance.[22] Another biblical theme, the call to national righteousness, was behind many other Nonconformist incursions into the public domain. A sense of responsibility for the corporate life of England drove many mid-century Non-conformists to join Anglicans in enforcing sabbath observance and opposing Roman Catholics. In both cases they felt attracted by the counter-arguments in favour of individual liberty, but they generally came down on the side of legislation against threats to the nation.[23] 'We are not such zealous *dissenters*,' announced *The Congregational Magazine* in 1845, 'as to forget we are *Protestants*'.[24] Again, on the temperance question, which steadily gained popularity in the chapels from the 1830s onwards, there was a shift from the initial concentration on moral suasion, which respected freedom of choice, towards also advocating prohibition, which did not. The United Kingdom Alliance, founded in 1853 to extinguish the trade in strong drink, drew an increasing number of Non-conformists towards seeing the state as a potential force for good in society.[25] The 'civic gospel' propagated by Non-conformist preachers in Birmingham from the middle of the century urged a parallel recognition of municipal authorities as agents of social improvement.[26] In foreign affairs, too, despite the wide currency of Richard Cobden's principle of non-interference, the prevailing Nonconformist opinion always allowed for Britain to take decisive military action abroad— during the Indian Mutiny, for instance.[27] In all these spheres the public stance of Nonconformity was shaped far less by beliefs about the supremacy of personal liberty than by other considerations—theological principle, zeal for public righteousness and straightforward patriotism. The

---

[22] Nigel Scotland, *Methodism and the Revolt of the Field* (Gloucester, 1981), p. 58, ch. 10.

[23] John Wigley, *The Rise and Fall of the Victorian Sunday* (Manchester, 1980), pp. 92-101. John Wolffe, *The Protestant Crusade in Great Britain, 1829–1860* (Oxford, 1991).

[24] *Congregational Magazine*, 1845, p. 397, quoted by Wolffe, *Protestant Crusade*, p. 204.

[25] Brian Harrison, *Drink and the Victorians: the temperance question in Engalnd, 1815–1872* (London, 1971), pp. 349, 365.

[26] E. P. Hennock, *Fit and Proper Persons: ideal and reality in nineteenth-century urban government* (London, 1973).

[27] Brian Stanley, 'Christian Responses to the Indian Mutiny of 1857', in W. J. Sheils, ed., *The Church and War* (Oxford, 1983), pp. 283-86.

socio-political outlook of the chapels was never simply
individualistic.

That is partly because the underlying religious attitudes did not
so dwell on the individual as to eclipse the community. Despite
what has already been said, Evangelicalism was itself ambiguous:
it called for souls to be saved one by one, and yet held up
standards of a just society that could often be imposed only at the
expense of individual freedom. Wesleyan Methodism, which
represented Evangelical religion without the libertarian heritage
of the Old Dissent, was always more inclined to endorse
sabbatarianism, anti-Catholicism and imperialism than the
Congregationalists or Baptists.[28] Likewise most branches of
Methodism (except the United Methodist Free Churches) held
aloof from the disestablishment crusade, and even from the
campaign for the redress of Nonconformist grievances, on the
ground that they did not want gospel work to be contaminated by
politics.[29] Methodism, that is to say, played virtually no part in the
public championship of individual religious liberties.
Furthermore, the religion of the chapels itself fostered a spirit of
community. Methodists were proud of their togetherness, the fruit
of frequent changes of preacher and a multiplicity of meetings.
'There is probably no body of Christians,' wrote a Wesleyan
apologist in 1879, 'that come into closer contact with each
other.'[30] But equally the churchmanship shared by Congregationalists and Baptists, according to which executive responsibility
might lie with minister and deacons but ultimate earthly authority
rested with the members gathered in Church Meeting, was a
powerful inducement to co-operative action blending individuals,
families and classes.[31] Since friendly societies generally served
alcohol and enjoyed semi-official patronage from the Church of

---

[28] Wigley, *Victorian Sunday*, p. 99. D. W. Bebbington, *The
Nonconformist Conscience: chapel and politics, 1870–1914* (London,
1982), pp. 92-93. S.E. Koss, 'Wesleyanism and Empire', *Historical
Journal*, 18 (1975).

[29] Kent, 'Methodism and Politics in the Nineteenth Century', *The
Age of Disunity* (London, 1966).

[30] *Methodism in 1879: impressions of the Wesleyan church and its
ministers* (London, 1879), p. 137.

[31] E.g., Clyde Binfield, *Pastors and People: the biography of a
Baptist Church. Queen's Road, Coventry* (Coventry, 1984), p. 56.

England,[32] many of their functions were commonly taken over by chapel auxiliaries. Most Nottinghamshire Baptist congregations, for example, had a provident society supplying basic insurance facilities.[33] Beyond the particular chapel, cousinhoods formed by marriage alliances and the working of denominational agencies forged long-distance linkages.[34] In consequence Nonconformists habitually thought in corporate terms. When, in 1881, Henry Allon addressed Con-gregationalists at the Jubilee Meeting of their Union, he identified individualism as their 'distinctive principle'. But a realisation of the responsibilities of individual life, he explained, created 'the truest sympathies of brotherhood and the most vital bond of union'.[35] In the heroic age of Nonconformity then closing, the liberty of the individual in life and conscience was indeed, as Helmstadter argues, a pillar of chapel social theory and of Old Dissenting political pressure. Yet at the same time, as he does not allow, family, workplace and the congregation itself induced social and political attitudes whose hallmark was corporate responsibility.

---

[32] James Obelkevich, *Religion and Rural Society: South Lindsey, 1825–1875* (Oxford, 1976), p. 89n.

[33] F. M. W. Harrison, 'The Nottinghamshire Baptists and Social Conditions', *Baptist Quarterly*, 27 (1978), p. 223.

[34] E.g., Clyde Binfield, *George Williams and the Y.M.C.A.: a study in Victorian social attitudes* (London, 1973), p. 35 (John Liefchild's connections).

[35] *Jubilee of the Congregational Union, Manchester, October 1881*, pp. 38-39, quoted in Binfield, *So Down to Prayers*, p. 26.

CHAPTER 5

Challenge and Decline

The last two decades of the nineteenth century, the stage at which
Nonconformist membership began to fall relative to population,
were also marked by significant changes of ethos in the chapels. It
would be wrong to exaggerate the sharpness of the turn, for there
was a high degree of continuity with what had passed before. In
particular, there was still much con-fidence, optimism and, in
many chapels, zeal for the salvation of souls. Yet ministers,
especially in inner-city areas, began to notice thinning
congregations. The drift to the suburbs, for all its benefits to the
new chapels built on the fringe of the growing cities, did great
harm to the older ones left in the centre. Even in a town such as
Reading, with well under 100,000 people, prosperous families
moving out deprived the central places of worship of their
initiative and largesse, and, by leaving the vicinity of their firms,
undermined the industrial deference from which the churches and
chapels alike had benefited.[1] In London, where clerks soon
followed their employers to the rising suburbs, the process was
often catastrophic. Up to the mid-1890s, for example, Shoreditch
Baptist Tabernacle in the East End of London enjoyed the support
of several well-to-do families, but, as it transferred them to
suburban chapels, the efforts of the minister, William Cuff, had to
be directed increasingly into money-raising. But the social
processes, as Cuff realised, were virtually irresistible. 'If you
make a man a Christian and a member of a Christian church,' he
explained, 'he steps into a new life, a new society, with higher
ideals than he has ever known. He becomes sober, thrifty,
respectable, in dress and everything. He will not live long in a
slum. So you lose him from the church and the neighbourhood.
There is so much salt and light gone from where it is badly

---

[1] Stephen Yeo, *Religion and Voluntary Organisations in Crisis*
(London, 1976).

needed.'[2] With the reduction of rural immigration to the cities in the closing years of the century, it has recently been suggested, the reservoir of chapel-minded people in the centre dried up, and so places like Shoreditch Tabernacle found it hard to recruit replacements.[3] Certainly the attractions of Nonconformist congregations for the working classes were diminishing. Board schools, technical schools and free public libraries were making the educational role of the chapels superfluous; welfare facilities such as public baths and the appearance of professional social workers began to undermine their philanthropic role, a development that was to be taken much further when the state entered the field in the Edwardian years.[4] Meanwhile alternative leisure activities— organised sport and the music hall being chief—were now widely available, and, from the 1890s, the rising tide of class consciousness was in some places drawing working men to Independent Labour meetings during chapel hours.[5] The social trends of the time were unpropitious for Nonconformity.

The chapels struggled nobly to respond. One technique was to take over some of the newly popular attractions and so to drop some of the traditional Evangelical taboos. In the past, for instance, football had been frowned on, and in some quarters it still was. When Thomas Waugh, a Wesleyan of the stricter holiness school, was preaching at a mission around 1890, the officials of the local football club feared that if the players were converted they would leave the team—which, Waugh adds in his account, 'thank the Lord! was exactly what happened'.[6] But more progressive Wesleyans actually promoted football clubs under chapel auspices, which is how Aston Villa, for example, was started. In Birmingham between 1871 and 1884 about 21% of cricket clubs and 25% of football clubs had religious affiliations,

[2] William Cuff, *Fifty Years' Ministry, 1865–1915: memories and musings* (London, 1915), p. 46.

[3] James Munson, *The Nonconformists: in search of a lost culture* (London, 1991), p. 301.

[4] Jeffrey Cox, *The English Churches in a Secular Society: Lambeth, 1870–1930* (Oxford, 1982), ch. 6.

[5] Peter Bailey, *Leisure and Class in Victorian England: rational recreation and the contest for control, 1830–1885* (London, 1978), chs 6 and 7. *Labour Leader*, 1 June 1895, p. 2.

[6] Thomas Waugh, *Twenty-Three Years a Missioner* (London, n.d.), pp. 221-22.

and many of them were Nonconformist.[7] Similarly, the Pleasant
Sunday Afternoon movement, which gathered force in the later
1880s, sought to hold religious services for working men that
were as entertaining as the music hall: they were advertised as
'Brief, Bright and Brotherly'.[8] 'Institutional Churches' were
founded to incorporate facilities for relaxation such as newspapers
and billiards, opportunities for choral singing and other musical
performances, and a variety of clubs within the life of the chapels.
The most notable, perhaps, was the series of central halls set up
from the mid-1880s by the Wesleyans as inner-city missions,
staffed by specially selected ministers released from the circuit
system and a team of lay assistants, some of them 'Sisters of the
People'.[9] Hugh Price Hughes, who presided over the best known
of these ventures, the West London Mission, was a daring
advocate of fresh thinking and fresh methods. Christians, he
contended, had been in the past too 'selfishly individualistic',[10]
but now they must throw themselves into the social causes that
appealed to the masses. That stance led him, for example, to
mediate in the London gas workers' strike of 1889, earning for
himself a stinging rebuke from its chairman.[11] Hughes and the
Baptist John Clifford were the leading advocates of a social
gospel, the chapels' call for justice in industrial society. Although
there were intellectual roots to this movement—it was partly a
response to Auguste Comte's Positivism[12]— it was primarily an
outgrowth of earlier public campaigns against prostitution and

----

[7] Tony Mason, *Association Football and English Society, 1863–1915*
(Brighton, 1980), p. 24. Cf. Hugh McLeod, '"Thews and Sinews":
Nonconformists and Sport in Nineteenth-Century England', in David
Bebbington and Timothy Larsen, ed., *Modern Christianity and Cultural
Aspirations* (London, 2003).

[8] K. S. Inglis, *Churches and the Working Classes in Victorian
England* (London, 1963), pp. 79-85.

[9] Inglis, *Churches and the Working Classes*, pp. 91-97.

[10] H. P. Hughes, *Social Christainity: sermons delivered in St James's
Hall* (London, 1889), p. xii. Cf. Christopher Oldstone-Moore, *Hugh
Price Hughes: founder of a new Methodism, conscience of a new
Nonconformity* (Cardiff, 1999).

[11] D. J. Jeremy, *Capitalists and Christians: business leaders and the
churches in Britain, 1900–1960* (Oxford, 1990), p. 157.

[12] D. M. Thompson, 'The Emergence of the Nonconformist Social
Gospel in England', in Keith Robbins, ed., *Protestant Evangelicalism:
Britain, Ireland, Germany and America, c.1750–c.1950: essays in
honour of W. R. Ward* (Oxford, 1990), pp. 270-73.

drunkenness. The social gospel demanded more effort by the state to combat a wide range of rampant national evils, and so fed into the New Liberalism, the anti-individualist trend of thought in the Edwardian Liberal Party. It was also taken up by many of the Free Church Councils that burgeoned in the 1890s.[13] The Nonconformists, like the political party that the great majority of them still supported, were seeing collectivism as a means of retaining the allegiance of the working classes.

Intellectual conditions also posed a serious challenge to Nonconformity, though not in the way that is often supposed. It is commonly said that a combination of Darwinian evolution and biblical criticism dealt a fatal blow to Evangelical belief in the later Victorian period, but that is not the case. Darwinism was almost painlessly assimilated by Nonconformist ministers, so that, for instance, in the early 1880s, the Queen's Road Baptist Young Men's Improvement Society in Coventry could listen to its pastor speaking 'on Darwin, the knowledge he had and love for the various kinds of flowers plants etc.'[14] One able Wesleyan minister, W. H. Dallinger, even turned evolutionary theory into a vehicle for Christian apologetic.[15] Likewise higher criticism of the Bible created little disturbance in Non-conformity, being accepted late, in the 1890s, but then remarkably smoothly.[16] Organised resistance to biblical criticism in any of the denominations emerged only in 1913, among a small group of Methodist Fundamentalists.[17] The chief solvent of Nonconformist theological conviction in the Victorian age was in fact the moral sensibility of the times. The Romantic epoch in England gave rise to certain views that tended to reinforce theological conservatism, especially the hope of an imminent second coming and the holiness teaching associated with the Keswick Convention, but

---

[13] D. W. Bebbington, *The Nonconformist Conscience: chapel and politics, 1870–1914* (London, 1982), chs 3 and 4.

[14] Clyde Binfield, *Pastors and People: the biography of a Baptist Church. Queen's Road, Coventry* (Coventry, 1984), p. 88.

[15] William Strawson, 'Methodist Theology, 1850–1950', in Rupert Davies *et al.*, ed., *A History of the Methodist Church in Great Britain*, 3 (London, 1983), p. 186.

[16] W. B. Glover, *Evangelical Nonconformists and Higher Criticism in the Nineteenth Century* (London, 1954).

[17] D. W. Bebbington, 'The Persecution of George Jackson: a British Fundamentalist controversy', in W. J. Sheils, ed., *Persecution and Toleration* (Oxford, 1984).

neither affected Nonconformity deeply in the Victorian period.[18]
What did sway Evangelical Nonconformists, particularly in Congregationalism, was the literary temper shaped by Thomas
Carlyle, Goethe and the English Romantic poets that found its
natural home among the Unitarians. Its leading Congregational
champion was James Baldwin Brown, whose *Divine Life in Man*
(1859) stressed the liberal themes of the Fatherhood of God, the
freedom of human nature and the imperative to righteousness.[19] A
Baptist divine of an older generation sternly denounced the book
as 'the first open inroad into English Evangelical Nonconformist
churches of a theology fatally deficient in the truth and power of
the gospel'.[20] As the milder theology gradually spread, the more
refined preachers began to leave out any mention of hell.[21]
Perhaps even more seriously for the future of Nonconformity, the
central place of the cross in the scheme of theology was usurped
in progressive circles by the incarnation. One of the distinctive
principles held by Evangelicals, a tenet that drove them to
outreach, was fading from view. Outspoken resistance to the
removal of the old landmarks by the doughty Calvinist C. H.
Spurgeon culminated in the Down Grade Controversy of 1887–
88, when he seceded from the Baptist Union amid a great furore.[22]
Yet the process of doctrinal erosion continued, gathering
momentum in the opening years of the twentieth century. The
convictions of many Nonconformists were becoming more
blurred.

The social and intellectual factors combined to bring on signs
of decay that were already very evident before the end of
Victoria's reign. Chapel debt had long been tolerated—
Shoreditch Tabernacle had paid 5% interest on a debt of £1,200

---

[18] Bebbington, *Evangelicalism in Modern Britain*, chs 3 and 5.

[19] Mark Hopkins, *Nonconformity's Romantic Generation:
Evangelical and liberal theologies in Victorian England* (Carlisle,
2004), ch. 2.

[20] J. H. Hinton, 'Strictures on some Passages in the Rev. J.B.
Brown's "Divine Life in Man"', *Baptist Magazine*, April 1860, p. 226.

[21] I. E. Page, ed., *John Brash: memorials and correspondence*
(London, 1912), p. 29. Cf. Michael Watts, *Why did the English stop
going to Church?*, 49th Friends of Dr Williams's Library Lecture
(London, 1995), which, however, exaggerates the role of the decline of
hell.

[22] Hopkins, *Nonconformity's Romantic Generation*, chs 5 and 7.

for thirty-six years[23] — but towards 1900 it probably scaled greater peaks, an indicator of improved building standards but also of declining generosity. Certainly obituaries laid increasing stress on the skills of ministers in raising money to pay off debts.[24] Likewise obituaries of Primitive Methodist laymen dwelt on their service to the cause rather than, as in the past, on their conspicuous piety.[25] Church discipline for moral or doctrinal offences became rarer and less public, a matter of pastoral guidance rather than formal excommunication.[26] Candidates for the ministry were less willing to acknowledge a definite conversion experience.[27] Traditional taboos were relaxed for reasons other than missionary effectiveness: whereas Henry Allon had been appointed to the Shakespeare Tercentenary Committee without ever having witnessed a play, theatre-going became respectable behaviour for late Victorian middle-class Nonconformists.[28] Chapel, especially in the sub-urbs, became less of an all-encompassing way of life, more one use of leisure among several. The slackening of community bonds had gone furthest in the Unitarian elite, where belief could sometimes shade away into reverent agnosticism. Joseph Chamberlain, though known as a Unitarian, attended the congregation where he was a member only twice in the nine years from 1894.[29] The extent of decay should not be exaggerated, for there were places such as the Durham colliery villages where Nonconformity was probably never stronger than around 1900.[30] But in circles where grammar or private school would often be followed by university, the younger generation increasingly saw no reason to identify with the despised Dissenters. There had always been a tendency for the most successful Nonconformists to move on to the parish church,

---

[23] Cuff, *Fifty Years' Ministry*, p. 28.

[24] K. D. Brown, *A Social History of the Nonconformist Ministry in England and Wales, 1800–1930* (Oxford, 1988), p. 143.

[25] James Obelkevich, *Religion and Rural Society: South Lindsey, 1825–1875* (Oxford, 1976), p. 252.

[26] Binfield, *Pastors and People*, p. 93.

[27] Brown, *Nonconformist Ministry*, pp. 50-53.

[28] W. H. Harwood, *Henry Allon, D.D.: pastor and teacher* (London, 1894), pp. 40-41.

[29] L. P. Jacks, *The Confession of an Octogenarian* (London, 1942), p. 153.

[30] Robert Moore, *Pit-Men, Preachers and Politics: the effects of Methodism in a Durham mining community* (Cambridge, 1974).

but from the end of Victoria's reign the trickle became a flood.[31]
The chapels were losing their grip on those who should have
replenished the pews and given leadership in the post-Victorian
period.

---

[31] Cox, *English Churches in a Secular Society*, ch. 7.

CHAPTER 6

Conclusion

The decline of Nonconformity was one of the most striking features of the social landscape in twentieth-century Britain. From 1906 onwards membership began to fall not just relative to population but in absolute terms. The twentieth century, ecclesiastically, was left in other hands. The story of English Christianity after 1920 has justifiably been depicted as a drift in a Catholic direction—towards Anglican High Churchmanship and Roman Catholicism.[1] Yet Victorian Nonconformists bequeathed a remarkable legacy to the following century. Although the Nonconformist conscience often concentrated narrowly on questions of personal behaviour (drinking, gambling and sexual immorality),[2] it inspired more than one generation of Free Churchmen and their offspring to see the world as an arena for the working out of high moral principles. Nonconformist MPs were far more numerous in the twentieth century than in the nineteenth. Furthermore, the religious tradition did not die. It was reinvigorated successively by Pentecostalists, charismatics within the denominations and house churches in parallel with them, so that by the period 1985–89 it was once more the Free Churches that were increasing while the Church of England and even in some measure the Roman Catholics were falling back.[3] The resurgence of these years was not subsequently sustained and the Nonconformist share of the overall population was much smaller than in the nineteenth century, but, at least for a while, the expanding sector of the movement was highly reminiscent of its

---

[1] Adrian Hastings, *A History of English Christianity, 1920–2000*, 4th edn (London, 2001).

[2] D. W. Bebbington, *The Nonconformist Conscience: chapel and politics, 1870–1914* (London, 1982), ch. 3.

[3] Peter Brierley, ed., *Prospects for the Nineties* (London, 1991), p. 20. Cf. D. W. Bebbington, 'Evangelism and Spirituality in Twentieth-Century Protestant Nonconformity', in A. P. F. Sell and A. R. Cross, ed., *Protestant Nonconformity in the Twentieth Century* (Carlisle, 2003).

Victorian predecessor. The salience of the chapels during the reign of Victoria had been based on a formula that in the 1980s seemed to have been rediscovered. Between 1837 and 1901 most of Nonconformity had a buoyancy that sprang from Evangelical belief; its denominational diversity allowed it to cater for different areas and social groups; it enjoyed advantages arising from its environment but relied chiefly on its own strategy of mission to achieve growth; and it maintained a delicate balance between a robust individualism and a well developed corporate sense. The chapels tried to embody the loftiest aspirations in a concrete pattern of social life that, for all its flaws and follies, gave fulfilment to millions. Victorian Nonconformity formed a vibrant Christian counter-culture.

Further Reading

General Studies

The most accessible introductory surveys of Victorian Nonconformity are R. J. Helmstadter, 'The Nonconformist Conscience', and Gerald Parsons, 'From Dissenters to Free Churchmen: the transitions of Victorian Nonconformity', in volumes 4 and 1 respectively of Parsons, ed., *Religion in Victorian Britain* (Manchester, 1988). James Munson, *The Nonconformists: in search of a lost culture* (London, 1991), is a fine study of the late Victorian and Edwardian Free Churches, while Ian Sellers, *Nineteenth Century Nonconformity* (London, 1977) is a succinct overview. Clyde Binfield has evoked the atmosphere of cultured Congregationalism in *So Down to Prayers: studies in English Nonconformity, 1780–1920* (London, 1977) and puts a congregation under the microscope in *Pastors and People: the biography of a Baptist Church: Queen's Road, Coventry* (Coventry, 1984). There are illuminating studies of the internal life of large Congregational churches in C. D. Cashdollar, *A Spiritual Home: life in British and American Reformed congregations, 1830–1915* (University Park, PA, 2000), and of theological issues in Mark Hopkins, *Nonconformity's Romantic Generation: Evangelical and liberal theologies in Victorian England* (Carlisle, 2004). The changing role of church leaders is analysed in K. D. Brown, *A Social History of the Nonconformist Ministry in England and Wales, 1800–1930* (Oxford, 1988). Geographical distribution is examined in Alan Everitt, *The Pattern of Rural Dissent: the nineteenth century* (Leicester, 1972), and in K. D. M. Snell, *Rival Jerusalems: the geography of Victorian religion* (Cambridge, 2000). Political themes are addressed in Timothy Larsen, *Friends of Religious Equality: Nonconformist politics in mid-Victorian England* (Woodbridge, Suffolk, 1999), and in D. W. Bebbington, *The Nonconformist Conscience: chapel and politics, 1870 1914* (London, 1982). There is an authoritative account of Welsh Nonconformity in R. T. Jones, *Faith and the Crisis of a Nation: Wales, 1890 1914* (Cardiff, 2004). Several collections of essays contain helpful studies: Jane Shaw and Alan Kreider, ed., *Culture and the Nonconformist Tradition* (Cardiff, 1999); David Bebbington and

Timothy Larsen, ed., *Modern Christianity and Cultural Aspirations* (London, 2003); and Timothy Larsen, *Contested Christianity: the political and social contexts of Victorian theology* (Waco, TX, 2004).

Broader Works

The earlier Nonconformist tradition is examined in M. R. Watts, *The Dissenters: from the Reformation to the French Revolution* (Oxford, 1978), and many nineteenth-century developments are covered in his *The Dissenters: Volume II: the expansion of Evangelical Nonconformity, 1791–1859* (Oxford, 1995). There are long-term perspectives in A. D. Gilbert, *Religion and Society in Industrial England: church, chapel and social change, 1740–1914* (London, 1976) and in D. W. Bebbington, *Evangelicalism in Modern Britain: a history from the 1730s to the 1980s* (London, 1989). The Evangelical context is set out in John Wolffe, *The Expansion of Evangelicalism: the age of Wilberforce, More, Chalmers and Finney* (Nottingham, 2006) and in D. W. Bebbington, *The Dominance of Evangelicalism: the age of Spurgeon and Moody* (Leicester, 2005). Rural religious practice is best illuminated in James Obelkevich, *Religion and Rural Society: South Lindsey, 1825–1875* (Oxford, 1976), and the urban scene in Hugh McLeod, *Class and Religion in the Late Victorian City* (London, 1974) and in Jeffrey Cox, *The English Churches in a Secular Society: Lambeth, 1870–1930* (New York, 1982). Revivalism is the subject of John Kent, *Holding the Fort: studies in Victorian revivalism* (London, 1978), of Richard Carwardine, *Transatlantic Revivalism: popular Evangelicalism in Britain and America, 1790–1865* (Westport, CT, 1978; Milton Keynes, 2006) and of Janice Holmes, *Religious Revivals in Britain and Ireland, 1859–1905* (Dublin, 2000). There is a suggestive study of social theory in Boyd Hilton, *The Age of Atonement: the influence of Evangelicalism on social and economic thought, 1785–1865* (Oxford, 1988); and G. I. T. Machin provides detailed political analyses in *Politics and the Churches in Great Britain, 1832–1868* (Oxford, 1977) and in *Politics and the Churches in Great Britain, 1869–1921* (Oxford, 1987).

Documents

There are two collections of documents about Nonconformity in John Briggs and Ian Sellers, ed., *Victorian Nonconformity* (London, 1973), and in D. M. Thompson, *Nonconformity in the Nineteenth Century* (London, 1972). A full sampling of documents will be found in D. W. Bebbington *et al.*, ed., *Protestant Nonconformist Texts: volume three: the nineteenth century* (Ashgate, 2006). There is a wider coverage in J. R. Moore, ed., *Religion in Victorian Britain*, vol. 3 (Manchester, 1988). On Methodism there are in addition R. Davies *et al.*, ed., *A History of the Methodist Church in Great Britain*, vol. 4 (London, 1988), and W. R. Ward, ed., *Early Victorian Methodism: the correspondence of Jabez Bunting, 1830–1858* (Oxford, 1976).

Particular Denominations

Studies of the various denominations are listed in the notes to chapter 2. A wealth of material may also be drawn from the periodicals of the Nonconformist historical societies: *The Baptist Quarterly*, *The Journal of the Friends' Historical Society*, the *Proceedings of the Wesley Historical Society* (for Methodists), *The Transactions of the Unitarian Historical Society* and *The Journal of the United Reformed Church History Society* (for Congregationalists, Presbyterians and the Churches of Christ).

Index